That We May Have Fellowship
Studies in First John

by John Lineberry

John Lineberry,
PS. 27:1

D1114679

REGULAR BAPTIST PRESS
SCHAUMBURG, ILLINOIS

Library of Congress Cataloging-in-Publication Data

Lineberry, John, 1926-
  That we may have fellowship.

  Bibliography: p.
  1. Bible. N.T.   John, 1st—Criticism, interpretation,
etc.   I. Title.
BS2805.2.L56   1986   227'.9406   86-24841
ISBN: 0-87227-115-3

To my beloved wife, Marjorie Alice,
full of faith and good works,
my God-given helpmeet and companion in life,
kind, gracious, understanding,
and a good mother to our children.
She has always encouraged me to do my best
for the glory of the blessed Savior.

Table of Contents

PREFACE

Fellowship with the Father, with the Lord Jesus and with one another is an ineffable spiritual privilege which delights and encourages our souls in the good things of the Lord. We learn about fellowship from the practical Word of God, which enriches and ennobles our lives as we believe its inspired truths and practice its trustworthy precepts.

The epistle of 1 John has much to say about fellowship, both with God and with other Christians. Fellowship with others is that sharing of the glories of redemptive grace, rejoicing together that we have been delivered from death, redeemed from ruin and saved from sin. Fellowship with others also includes sharing each other's burdens and trials. Of course, the prerequisite to fellowship with other believers is "that ye love one another."

First John challenges us to please the Lord by walking with Him in yielded obedience and surrendered service—this is fellowship with God. As we continue in this fellowship, we grow in grace and mature in the things of Christ.

These studies in 1 John are sent forth prayerfully to encourage God's people to honor the Lord always in thought, word and deed.

John Lineberry
Silvis, Illinois

CHAPTER I
INTRODUCTION

Every believer ought to thank and praise the Lord for the epistle of 1 John, since it tells of the wonderful provisions God has made for us to experience and enjoy the greatest of all spiritual exercises, namely, fellowship with God. This fellowship brings joyous glory to our souls, assuring us of daily power and victory in our lives as we walk in dependence upon the Holy Spirit, Who gives enabling grace and strength.

Before we begin an actual study of the letter, it will be profitable to look at some historical facts, as well as noting some things about the inspired penman—the apostle John. The date of the epistle is commonly put at A.D. 90, or about six years before the book of Revelation; hence, it was written before John's trying banishment to the Isle of Patmos.

The letter is addressed to no particular church or individual. It is thought by some that the apostle had in mind a group of churches, such as, perhaps, the seven churches of Asia (Rev. 1:11).

Quite likely, the Christian addressees were mostly of Gentile rather than Jewish origin. The basis for that conclusion is that there are few references to the Old Testament; also there are allusions such as that of 1 John 5:21, "Little children, keep yourselves from idols."

John is often referred to as the apostle of love, as Paul is

the apostle of grace and Peter the apostle of hope. John was
the beloved disciple, the son of Zebedee, brother of James
the elder (Matt. 4:21). He is that disciple who without mention of name is spoken of in the fourth Gospel as especially
dear to the Lord Jesus (John 13:23).

In Matthew 4:18-21 there is recorded the Lord's call for
service (not for salvation) of Peter and Andrew and John and
his brother James from the sea and from the nets. The
Master's call was twofold:

1. "Follow me," meaning literally, "Be walking the same
road with me" and

2. "I will make you fishers of men," defining the holy work
of God in and through His servants—"I will cause you to
catch men alive."

This, then, is the successful key to Christian witness and
service—bringing dying men to the living Savior.

It is little wonder that John, along with James, Peter and
Andrew, at once left the sea and the nets to catch men alive
for Christ. What indescribable joy it is to engage in the most
wonderful and enduring business in all the world.

Let us now get back to the epistle itself.

> The occasion and object of its writing seem to have
> been furnished by the presence of false teachers, as we
> may judge from many passages, of which 2:18-26 and
> 4:6 are examples. And indeed, as a matter of fact, we
> learn from the writers of church history that very ear-
> ly there were three classes of heretics, as they were
> called: (1) Ebionites, who denied the deity of Christ; (2)
> the Docetists, who denied His humanity; (3) the Cerin-
> thians, who denied the union of the two natures,
> human and divine, prior to His baptism.[1]

The two latter groups were Gnostics. Much more will be
said about them later, but for now we need to remember that
they were a group that laid claim to superior knowledge. Let
us keep in mind that all false doctrine, ancient or modern,

sooner or later denies either the Person or the work of Christ.

The book of 1 John breaks down into four general divisions:

We will begin here with the **introduction**.

> *1 John 1:1.* That which was from the beginning, which we have heard, which we have seen with our eyes, which we have looked upon, and our hands have handled, of the Word of life.

The words "that which was from the beginning" remind us at once of John's Gospel, in which John 1:1 declares three truths about the Lord Jesus:

1. His eternality, "In the beginning was the Word"
2. His distinct Person, "and the Word was with (lit. "facing," speaking of fellowship and equality) God (the Father)" and
3. His sinless deity, "and the Word was God," or, as it is in the original for emphasis, "and God was the Word."

All of which means that our Lord was not a creature of God, not an *aeon* as the Gnostics affirmed, but the eternal Son of God.

The proponents of the docetic (from the Greek *dokeō*, "to seem," "to think") heresy denies Christ's humanity, saying that His body was only a phantom, that He seemed to have a body but that it was not real.

There is a sane, sensible, Scriptural answer to the wild, senseless, ridiculous opinions of men. The inspired Record proves that the Lord Jesus' real and true humanity is based upon irrefutable facts, for His disciples "heard Him," "saw

Him" and "handled Him." The Scriptures forcefully declare
the humanity of our Lord to be real indeed, and the Docet-
ists' guesses and opinions were, therefore, wrong and misleading.

> *1 John 1:2.* For the life was manifested, and we have
> seen it, and bear witness, and shew unto you that eter-
> nal life, which was with the Father, and was manifest-
> ed unto us.

The words "the life was manifested" declare that God has
revealed Himself in the Person of His Son. God has con-
descended in grace from the highest heights in Heaven to
show His all-sufficient provisions of redeeming love for our
salvation.

The words "bear witness" proclaim powerfully that we
have a story of life to tell and a blessed Person to present to
dying men. Moses said, "I will publish the name of the
LORD..." (Deut. 32:3). Like a physician with medicine for
healing, we are to get out the message of the gospel because
it is a sure, proved cure for the sin-sick soul.

The statement in 1 John 1:2, "that eternal life, which was
with the Father," announces that our Lord and Savior belongs rightly to eternity, being the "Ancient of days" (Dan.
7:22); "whose goings forth have been of old, from everlasting
(lit. 'from the days of eternity')" (Micah 5:2); Who had glory
with the Father before the creation of the world (John 17:5).

Man is born, lives a few fleeting years, and then dies—all
within the bounded limits of time. But God is eternal—
timeless, before time, after time, above time. What a refreshing truth to know that God is without beginning or end.
When it comes to the question of eternity no one but God can
answer it. Jesus is eternal and, being eternal, He is God
"manifested unto us," assuring us that we can be rightly
related to the endlessness of eternity only as we are rightly
related to Him through redemptive grace. He is the sure indestructible Rock of our salvation—for time and eternity.

> *1 John 1:3.* That which we have seen and heard declare we unto you, that ye also may have fellowship with us: and truly our fellowship is with the Father, and with his Son Jesus Christ.

To be sure, the gospel is not a secret to be hidden, nor is it a puzzling, religious enigma needing esoteric deciphering. It is a thrilling, dynamic, life-giving, soul-transforming message to be proclaimed. "That which we have seen and heard declare we unto you."

To preach the gospel is to present Christ. To receive Christ by faith is to become a living possessor of eternal life and to enter into fellowship with the Father and with His Son the Lord Jesus. To fellowship with God is an amazing spiritual privilege.

The term "fellowship" is an important key word in 1 John. We need to know more about it so that our experience may equal our understanding. Today the word "fellowship" simply means "social intercourse." It is rather difficult to formulate any real meaning for so broad a term in modern English. Originally, however, the word was not used so broadly and loosely. The Greek word is *koinonia,* connoting primarily "joint-participation," or, used in an ancient sentence, "belonging in common to." The word has in it the thought of sharing or partnership.

We hardly need to mention that there are some essentials to fellowship.

1. There must be a common life or nature.
2. There must be common likes or dislikes.
3. The person with whom we have sweet fellowship must be seen and known.

How does the gospel meet those needs for us to fellowship with God?

1. Believers have the life of God in Christ by grace (Eph. 2:8); therefore, fellowship is possible.
2. God's nature in us causes us to love righteousness and hate evil (2 Pet. 1:4), making fellowship with God possible.

3. We see the Lord Jesus through the eyes of faith (Gal. 3:1), through "Holy Spirit ground lenses," and we know Him through the provisions of redemptive mercy (John 17:3; 1 John 5:11-13); hence, fellowship with God is real, resulting in our abiding joy and strength.

> *1 John 1:4.* And these things write we unto you, that your joy may be full.

The fruit of fellowship is joy. The word "write" means that the message of life is preserved undiminished in the sure, infallible, inspired lines of Holy Scripture for our spiritual growth, comfort, edification and joy.

The Lord desires that our gladness of heart be full, complete. There will be an abundance of blessing as we feast upon the truth that our joy in Christ is lasting, satisfying and running over. "But whosoever drinketh of the water that I shall give him shall never thirst; but the water that I shall give him shall be in him a well of water springing up into everlasting life" (John 4:14).

The wells of the world, filled with the devil's poison, offer a false satisfaction to our thirst, and the drawers thereof are bound to come sooner or later to bewilderment and frustration. But the thirst-quenching water of the gospel brings complete satisfaction to our souls.

CHAPTER II
RESOURCES FOR FELLOWSHIP

In our study, we need to keep two distinct truths fixed clearly in our minds:

1. The bond in Christ by grace in salvation is so strong that nothing can break it.

2. Our fellowship with God is so fragile that the very slightest sin can interrupt it.

This latter statement does not mean, however, that we are to give up at the start, giving way to discouragement and failing even to put forth a good honest effort. Instead, we are to be much encouraged in view of the truth that God has made the resources available for His people to live in constant, enjoyable fellowship with Him.

While the grace of God has supplied these resources for us, the whole general tenor of Scripture teaches us that there are certain conditions that we must meet for blessing. This was true of Israel in the Old Testament. It is true of us now in this age.

Now we will begin to examine the second division of 1 John, **fellowship with God in light.**

> *1 John 1:5.* This then is the message which we have heard of him, and declare unto you, that God is light, and in him is no darkness at all.

Fellowship with God is maintained as we walk in the light,

appropriating the provisions of God's grace.

The word for "message" is *aggelia*—"announcement," "thing announced," "precept declared." The writer continues by saying that the inspired message had been "heard of him," a construction indicating that Christ was the source as well as the subject of the message. Since the message is from Him, it is trustworthy, authoritative and inspired. ". . . The words that I speak unto you," said the Lord Jesus, "they are spirit, and they are life" (John 6:63).

Often, for spiritual strength and comfort, we must come back to the very basic truth that the message is from God. Therefore, all the modernist's apostasy, all the atheist's unbelief, all the infidel's disregard, all the agnostic's ignorance cannot, shall not ever militate against the revealed Word of God anymore than a hummingbird could divert the course of an eagle in flight.

The changing philosophies of men will fail, but, "For ever, O LORD, thy word is settled in heaven" (Ps. 119:89). The same wonderful truth is expressed in 1 Peter 1:25, "But the word of the Lord endureth for ever. . . ." Let us now and always remember that the message is from God. He has decreed its perpetuity. The enemy will not steal one cup from its ocean of truth or pluck one flower from its garden of beauty. God Himself has declared for us blessings in His Word. Like the refreshing rains in summer's drought which fill the air with renewed freshness, so does the Word of God revive, cleanse and bless us, stirring our hearts to obedience and service.

The contextual message is that "God is light," words clothed with spiritual power. Though short and simple, they speak thrilling and uplifting truth, since:

> Light unites in itself purity, clearness, beauty, and glory, as no other material object does. It is the condition of all material life, growth and joy. The application to God means that He is light, the fountain of light material and spiritual. In the one world, darkness is the absence of light; in the other, darkness, untruthful-

ness, deceit, falsehood, is the absence of God. They
who are in communion with God, and walk with God,
are of the light, and walk in the light.[1]

We are not, of course, to understand that light is the sum
total of the being of God, but rather that light is a revealed at-
tribute of God, an inherent quality in His nature that helps
us to know Him.

What a refreshing truth—"God is light." What sobering,
sense-giving, soul-searching words—"in him is no darkness
at all." Surely words fail to describe the appalling wickedness of the thinking that one can be associated with God on
the one hand and with evil on the other at the same time.
"For thou art not a God that hath pleasure in wickedness:
neither shall evil dwell with thee" (Ps. 5:4).

> *1 John 1:6.* If we say that we have fellowship with him,
> and walk in darkness, we lie, and do not the truth.

It is a generally understood principle of the Word of God
that what we do must not belie what we say. Our conduct
must be in step with our creed. Fundamentalists are sometimes accused of being long on precept and short on practice.
The sad part about the whole accusation is that it is sometimes true. This is inexcusable since God has made provisions for our walk to be an honest, outward expression of
our doctrine. Orthodoxy is sound doctrine. Orthopraxy is
right life. Both are needed simultaneously and consistently.
Both must walk together, hand in hand.

Verse 6 issues a stern warning to the antinomians of that
day as well as to compromisers of this day. "Antinomianism" means literally, "against law." It was that teaching that
said, in effect, that a person may be living in sin, compromising with it, and at the same time enjoying fellowship with
God. What a very wicked teaching, indeed! Even the casual
student of Scripture can discern that antinomianism is foreign to the truth of God's Word. The Nicolaitanes of Revelation 2:6 were early antinomians.

The words "If we say" demand careful consideration, lest we divert and twist the truth and read into the text what *is not* there, instead of lifting out of the text what *is* there. When the word "we" comes before us in John's first epistle, we say that it refers to Christians, saved individuals, since the whole general context of the letter is addressed to believers. While that is true, there still must be a closer look at the words in view of the fact that the antinomian boasted in one breath that he was in fellowship with God, and in the next that he was living in sin.

The words "If we say" are a deliberative subjunctive, a construction that proposes a hypothetical case. The inspired writer:

> put the case as a supposition, not an assumed fact. He deals gently and humbly with his readers including himself in the statement. The claim of this hypothetical person is that he is having fellowship with God (p. 101)[2].

"Walk" is *peripateō*, compounded of *peri*, "around," and *pateō*, "to walk." The full meaning of the word is "to walk around." The reader can readily see how the word soon came to mean "to make one's way"; hence, "to regulate one's life," "to conduct oneself." So the word is used in the New Testament to refer to one's behavior or conduct. The verb "to walk" is in the present tense, which speaks of habitual or continuous action.

> Thus, this person (Antinomian—lawless one), is sinning habitually, continuously, which shows that he is an unsaved person. No child of God sins habitually to the exclusion of righteous acts. We learn that from John's use of modes and tenses as we proceed in our exegesis of this Epistle (p. 101).

"Darkness" is from *skotia*, used in reference to the one who is ignorant of divine things, and the associated wickedness of this ignorance and the resultant misery.

The final words of the verse, ". . . we lie, and do not the truth," are a further description of the person who claims to be in fellowship with God while ordering his behavior in darkness. His actions and words are encircled by sin. Nothing of God's righteousness or goodness ever enters that circle. The person is unsaved, to be sure, since "none can have fellowship with Him who walk in darkness."[3]

> *1 John 1:7.* But if we walk in the light, as he is in the light, we have fellowship one with another, and the blood of Jesus Christ his Son cleanseth us from all sin.

The believer's fellowship with God is this walking in the light. The obedient child of God is blessed as he walks with the Lord.

"Now John supposes another case, that of a person walking in the sphere of the light which God is and in which He dwells" (KSW, 101). The words "we" and "us" in verse 7 refer to believers. Again the word "walk" is from *peripateō*, as in verse 6 above. The word means "to conduct oneself," "to order one's behavior." The verb construction speaks of continuous action. The habitual actions of an individual express his real character. The Christian who constantly walks in the sphere of the light which God is and in which He dwells demonstrates outwardly the inward work of God in the soul.

Obedience to our Lord in our daily walk makes sweet and blessed fellowship a glorious reality, for the Word teaches us, ". . .Behold, to obey is better than sacrifice, and to hearken than the fat of rams" (1 Sam. 15:22).

To whom does the statement "one with another" refer in verse 7? The words do not have reference to the lawless ones of verse 6 who do not have salvation and are, therefore, incapable of any real sharing of divine things. The words "one with another" do not refer to the fellowship of Christians one with another, in spite of the fact that this is the commonly accepted interpretation. In Greek the words are a reciprocal pronoun, which makes the meaning unmistakably clear that the fellowship is between God and the Christian. That interpretation best suits the general theme of the entire epistle, which is fellowship with God. What wonderful glory and blessing that the almighty Sovereign of the universe should condescend in mercy to fellowship with us, sinners saved by grace!

But wait a moment; there is more, ". . . and the blood of Jesus Christ his Son cleanseth us from all sin." Here is the truth that:

> . . . while we are having this fellowship with Him, the blood of Jesus, His Son, keeps on constantly cleansing us from sins of omission, sins of ignorance, sins we know nothing about in our lives and for the reason that we have not grown in grace enough to see that they are sin. These would prevent our fellowship with God if this divine provision of the constant cleansing away of the defilement of sin in our lives was not taken care of by the blood of the Lord Jesus Christ. So holy is the God with whom we have fellowship (KSW, 101).

CHAPTER III
CONDITIONS OF FELLOWSHIP

1 John 1:8. If we say that we have no sin, we deceive ourselves, and the truth is not in us.

To deceive oneself on this matter of indwelling sin does not alter the teaching of Scripture about it. The teaching of sinless perfection, or the eradication of the totally depraved nature, sometimes referred to as the dying out completely of the old man, is an erroneous illusion foreign to Scripture.

One's earnest convictions cannot negate the Scriptural truth that the teaching of sinless perfection is not found anywhere in the Bible. Even the voice of our own experience cries out against the twisting of the truth that the old Adamic nature, inherited from the federal head of the whole human race (Rom. 5:12), here and now is uprooted completely. It might be said also in passing that the ancient Gnostics held that we do not have any principle of sin in us. They taught that matter is evil and the soul is not contaminated by sinful flesh.

If the verse under consideration teaches anything it is that the unscriptural teaching of sinless perfection thrives on ignorance, borne out by the words "we deceive ourselves, and the truth is not in us." That ignorance is twofold:

1. There is ignorance about the true nature of sin.
2. There is ignorance about the real meaning of "justification" and "sanctification." Justification is often referred to

as the "first blessing" and sanctification the "second bless-ing." It is not the purpose of this study to go into an exhaus-tive discussion of those great doctrinal words. Perhaps we should say here that sanctification cannot refer to sinless-ness since objects, which have no sin, are said to be sancti-fied. For example, the tabernacle of old was sanctified (Exod. 29:43). The basic meaning of the verb "to sanctify" is "to set apart." By no stretch of the imagination can that meaning be enlarged to teach sinless perfection.

The "we" and "us" of 1 John 1:8 again have reference to believers, and "we" get along best and progress in grace most rapidly by admitting the presence of sin in "us" and by appropriating the provisions of God for cleansing and for-giveness.

The word for sin is *hamartia*, here without the definite ar-ticle, and has reference to the sin nature rather than acts of sin. The next words in the verse are "we deceive ourselves." In other words, if we deny the presence of the old sin nature in us, we lead ourselves astray. Christians who believe that the totally depraved nature, passed down from Adam, is eradicated in this life, deceive no one but themselves, as shown by the emphatic position of the pronoun "ourselves." The emphatic position means that it stands first in the sen-tence, a grammatical device used by the Greeks to register emphasis. Everybody else can see sin written all over us in our experience, and acts of sin must proceed from the source of the indwelling sinful nature. We cannot deceive those who truly know us.

The remaining words in 1 John 1:8 are "and the truth is not in us." What is the meaning of these words?

> In the case of the Gnostics that statement must be taken in an absolute sense. They were unsaved. In the case of a misinformed and mistaken present-day Christian, the statement will have to be qualified to mean that the truth of the indwelling sinful nature is not in him. The context would require this interpreta-tion (KSW, 104).

> *1 John 1:9.* If we confess our sins, he is faithful and just
> to forgive us our sins, and to cleanse us from all un-
> righteousness.

God has made adequate provision for taking care of sins in our lives. In rightly dividing the Word, one should remember that sinners are saved by believing the gospel (John 3:16; 20:31; Eph. 1:13), while saints are forgiven by confessing their sins to God.

The word "confess" is from *homologeō*, compounded of *homos*, "one and the same," and *legō*, "to say." The full meaning is "to say the same thing as another," or "to agree with another," therefore, "to admit the truth of an accusation" as seen clearly in King David's confession, "Against thee, thee only, have I sinned, and done this evil in thy sight: that thou mightest be justified when thou speakest, and be clear when thou judgest" (Ps. 51:4).

> Confession of sin on the part of the saint means therefore to say the same thing that God does about that sin, to agree with God as to all the implication of that sin as it relates to the Christian who commits it and to a holy God against whom it is committed. That includes the saint's hatred of that sin, his sense of guilt because of it, his contrition because of it, the deter-mination to put it out of his life and never to do that thing again. This is what confession of sin means here (KSW, 104).

The verb "confess" is present tense, speaking of contin-uous action. This teaches that the constant attitude of the saint toward sin should be one of a contrite heart, ever eager to have any sin in the life discovered for him by the Holy Spirit, and ever eager to confess it and put it out of his life by the glorious power available through the Holy Spirit. Scrip-ture says, "The sacrifices of God are a broken spirit: a broken and a contrite heart, O God, thou wilt not despise" (Ps. 51:17). I once heard a noted Bible teacher comment, "The way to victory is to keep short accounts with God."

It is generally believed that a failure to understand fully what genuine, deep-rooted confession of sin involves has helped produce a generation of believers who view sin too lightly, an attitude that results in spiritual decadence. To view sin lightly is gross flagrance and results in that which is spiritually harmful, for, "He that covereth his sins shall not prosper: but whoso confesseth and forsaketh them shall have mercy" (Prov. 28:13); and "If I regard [look with favor upon] iniquity in my heart, the Lord will not hear me" (Ps. 66:18).

If there is one thing that needs to be said over and over again to God's people, it is that forgiveness of sin is not realized by a half-hearted, unconcerned, flippant confession of sin. There must be deep heart-searching, genuine godly sorrow and a radical turning away from sin for the child of God to receive forgiveness. All of those weighty words are involved in the Scriptural meaning of confession.

Our churches across the country are yearning for revival. Surely some Christians are missing God's best by hanging on to their wicked sins. There are no short cuts to revival. When we get down to business in heartfelt, life-changing, Holy Spirit produced confession of sins to God, the fire from Heaven will fall, the blessings of revival will come according to the promises of God in His Word (2 Chron. 7:14—God's one formula for revival), and sinners will then be saved. Then the grace of God will triumph in the souls of men.

The use of the plural "sins" in 1 John 1:9 indicates that the confession is to be specific as well as general. There are two things said about God in His forgiveness of our sins, conditioned, of course, upon our confession:

1. He is faithful.
2. He is just.

"Faithful" means that God is true to His own nature and promises, keeping faith with Himself and with man. The word is applied to God as fulfilling His own promises (Heb. 10:23; 11:11). The word also means that God is faithful to His Son, our Savior, Who died for us upon the cross, thereby providing the resources for forgiveness.

"Just," rendered by the Revised "righteous," is *dikē*, "right," a term which is applied both to God and to Christ. The two words "faithful" and "righteous" imply each other. They unite in a true conception of God's character. God, Who is absolute rightness, must be faithful to His own nature, and His righteous dealing with men who partake of that nature and walk in fellowship with Him is simply fidelity to Himself. Righteousness is truth passing into action (Vincent cited by KSW, 105).

The word "forgive" means "to remit as a debt," "to put away," "to send away," "to dismiss." Upon confession of our sins, God sends them away, dismisses them from us. The verb tense shows that these sins for which confession is required are infrequent, isolated instances in the well-ordered life of a believer. To be sure, no child of God knowingly sins habitually.

"Cleanse" translates *katharizō*, "to make clean," "to pronounce clean," showing that God cleanses the believer from the defilement he incurred in committing the act of sin. Again the verb tense of the word speaks of a single act of cleansing, for known sin in the life of a saint is not habitual but out of the ordinary.

The final word in the verse is "unrighteousness," which renders *adikias*. The usage of this word here shows that the righteous One, Who calls us into fellowship with Himself, purges away the unrighteousness which is contrary to His nature and which renders fellowship impossible.

> *1 John 1:10.* If we say that we have not sinned, we make him a liar, and his word is not in us.

In verse 8, it is the indwelling sinful nature that is denied. In verse 10, specific sins are denied. The words, "we have not sinned," are in the perfect tense, which tense refers to an action completed in the past, having present results. The specific function of that tense here is to show that there was a

denial of any acts of sin committed in the past with the impli-
cation that none are able to be committed at present. I recall
that Dr. Kenneth S. Wuest said once in class, "Such a denial
of sins amounts to the claim of sinless perfection with a ven-
geance."

It is a serious thing for one to claim that he has not sinned.
Such a brazen statement makes God a liar, and John says
that person does not have the Word of God in him. Here is a
good summary of those words:

> Perfectionism has two causes:
> 1. the stifling of conscience: we make Him a liar, *i.e.*,
> turn a deaf ear to His inward testimony, His voice in
> our souls;
> 2. ignorance of His Word: it "is not in us." Such a delu-
> sion were impossible if we steeped our minds in the
> Scripture (Smith cited by KSW, 107).

CHAPTER IV
OUR LORD'S INTERCESSORY MINISTRY

1 John 2:1. My little children, these things write I unto you, that ye sin not. And if any man sin, we have an advocate with the Father, Jesus Christ the righteous.

Since learning begins with definition, let us examine the word "advocacy." By the advocacy of Jesus Christ for sinning saints we mean that work that He carries on with the Father by which He restores them to fellowship (Ps. 23:3; John 13:10). It is a thrilling truth of Scripture that our Lord pleads our case at the throne of God.

In the previous chapters, we examined the subjects of fellowship with the Father, the conditions of that fellowship and hindrances to fellowship. Now let us dig deeper into the epistle of 1 John to view a different aspect of fellowship, wherein we see our Savior as our High Priest at the throne of grace (Heb. 4:14-16).

The words "My little children" in 1 John 2:1 form a special term of endearment from the aged apostle. The designation "children" translates *teknia*, meaning "born ones," hence, children of grace, born of the Holy Spirit, with emphasis upon the true, genuine aspect of the relationship with God in salvation. In God's sight, to be sure, we are "little born ones," therefore always utterly dependent upon His sustaining grace every step of our pilgrim journey.

The word "children" is a favorite with John because it

denotes our nearness to the Father, our God, Who is our Keeper and Upholder. Paul employs another word, *huios* (Greek "son"), quite frequently to show our public position to God as sons through the free bestowal of salvation.

Our filial position before the Father is a very precious one, effected by the regenerating power of the Holy Spirit. Let us, then, remind ourselves that we are not born again by our own works (Isa. 64:6), but by the grace of God (Eph. 2:8, 9; Titus 3:5), which is given freely and lavished abundantly in our hearts through the miracle of redeeming mercy.

The contextual exhortation to the little children follows: ". . . These things write I unto you, that ye sin not. And if any man sin, we have an advocate with the Father. . . ." The kind of verb construction used in ". . . if any man sin . . ." speaks not of habitual action but of a single act. It could better be rendered ". . .if any man commit an act of sin." John regards sin in the believer's life not as habitual but as extraordinary, as infrequent.

Without getting too technically involved in this kind of study, one might safely say that God's ideal is that His children sin not. In the very next words, however, God tells us ". . . and if any man sin, we have an advocate with the Father. . . ." Believers must never forget that they are still in the flesh!

What is the meaning of the words, ". . . that ye sin not. And if any man sin . . ."? "John has no patience with professional perfectionists (1:8-10), but he has still less with loose-livers like some of the Gnostics who went to all sorts of excesses without shame."[1]

Further, those words can be illustrated by the following:

> As a physician might say to his patient: "Your trouble is obstinate; the poison is in your blood, and it will take a long time to eradicate it. But I do not tell you this to discourage you or make you careless; no, on the contrary, to make you watchful and diligent in the use of the remedy"; so the Apostle says, "My little children,

these things I am writing to you in order that ye may not sin."[2]

If, however, we fall into sin, let us not lose heart in view of the fact that ". . . we have an advocate with the Father. . . ." The word for advocate is *paraklētos*, "one called to your side," used especially in a forensic sense, "one who undertakes and champions your cause." The word is also used in John 14:16, 26; 15:26; 16:7 in reference to the Holy Spirit. "The Holy Spirit is God's Advocate on earth with men, while Christ is man's Advocate with the Father."[3].

Our Advocate is with the Father in Heaven, exalted triumphantly to the right hand of the Majesty in Glory (Heb. 1:3). What a comforting benediction to know that our Advocate is "with" the Father. "With" renders *pros*, better translated "facing" the Father.

> Our Advocate is always in fellowship with the Father in order that if the saint loses fellowship with Him through cherished and unconfessed sin, He might plead our cause on the basis of His precious blood, and bring us back into fellowship again. The word "facing" brings us to this solemn thought, that when we saints sin, the Lord Jesus must face the Father with us and our sin. The saint has been saved in His precious blood so that he may be able to keep from sinning and when he does sin he wounds the tender heart of the Savior, and forces Him to face God the Father with that saint whom He has saved in His precious blood. How that should deter us from committing acts of sin (KSW, 109, 110).

The remaining words of 1 John 2:1 identify our Advocate, "Jesus Christ, the righteous (one)." Our Advocate is not an angel, a priest, a preacher, some religious pundit, a church or a denomination; but, thank God, He is Jesus Christ the righteous One, Who alone is qualified to plead our case and to enter the Father's presence (Heb. 2:18).

1 John 2:2. And he is the propitiation for our sins: and not for ours only, but also for the sins of the whole world.

The scope of God's redemptive mercy is as wide as the scope of the guilt of sin. The gospel call for salvation goes out to all the people of the whole world.

The word "propitiation" is from *hilasmos,* one of the great words of fundamental Christianity. It comes from the verb *hilaskomai,* which in pagan usage meant "to appease," "to conciliate to oneself," "to make a god propitious to one."

> However, when the word comes over into New Testament usage, its meaning is radically changed ... the scriptural conception of the verb is not that of appeasing one who is angry with a personal feeling against the offender; but of altering the character of that which, from without, occasions a necessary alienation, and interposes an inevitable obstacle to fellowship. Such phrases as "propitiating God," and "God being reconciled" are foreign to the language of the New Testament (KSW, 110).

Every earnest Bible student knows that sin was the cause of the alienation between God and man.

> It was the guilt of sin that separated man from his Creator. Our Lord on the cross assumed that guilt and paid the penalty in His own blood, and thus removed the cause of alienation. Now a holy and righteous God can bestow mercy upon a believing sinner on the basis of justice satisfied. Our Lord provided a satisfaction for the demands of the broken law. That satisfaction is the *hilasmos,* propitiation. The Greek has it, "He Himself is a satisfaction." The intensive pronoun is used. The point is that the Old Testament priest offered an animal sacrifice, but not himself as the sacrifice. This wonderful New Testament Priest is both the priest and the sacrifice (KSW, 110, 111).

The remaining words of 1 John 2:2, ". . . for our sins: and not for ours only, but also for the sins of the whole world" emphasize forcefully the Bible truth that Christ died for all individuals, and that anyone who wants to be saved can be saved through personal faith and trust in the finished work of Christ upon the cross. Luther said, "It is a patent fact that thou too are a part of the whole world: so that thine heart cannot deceive itself and think, the Lord died for Peter and Paul, but not for me."

CHAPTER V
TESTS OF FELLOWSHIP

1 John 2:3. And hereby we do know that we know him, if we keep his commandments.

The marvelous, inexhaustible, wonderful, justifying, sanctifying, glorifying grace of God received in the soul has an inevitable way of expressing itself in the life of the believer through obedience. The Scriptures declare, ". . . Behold, to obey is better than sacrifice, and to hearken than the fat of rams" (1 Sam. 15:22b).

Someone asked a well-known Bible scholar, "What translation of the Bible do you like best?" He answered, "That one by my mother!" "Oh," the inquirer replied, "I was not aware that your mother had made a translation." The scholar continued, "I refer to the translation that my mother puts into everyday life and practice."

Our daily walk of loving obedience pleases the heart of God as nothing else possibly ever could. Of course, sound doctrine and right life are important to Christians in any age, especially in our own time.

The word "know," used two times in the verse, is from *ginoskō* and refers to "knowledge gained by experience." It is that experiential knowledge gained from the living experiences of keeping His commandments, which are kept as we read and study the Word of God, pray, witness and render spiritual service to our blessed Lord as the Holy Spirit bestows enabling grace upon us.

One of the tremendous needs for these perilous times is for God's people to put their faith into living action. Today we need more going on the promises and less sitting on the premises. Wonderful blessings indeed accrue to us in knowing the Savior in heart and living for Him in life—spiritual exercises that bring unwavering assurance to our souls.

The word "keep" is from *tereō*, "to attend to carefully," "to guard," "to observe." Living for the Master demands the very best that is in us as we attend carefully to spiritual matters, keeping our Lord's Word and doing His perfect will. "The Gnostics boasted of their superior knowledge of Christ, and John here challenges their boast by an appeal to experimental knowledge of Christ which is shown by keeping His commandments."[1]

> *1 John 2:4.* He that saith, I know him, and keepeth not his commandments, is a liar, and the truth is not in him.

Matthew 15:8 reads, "This people draweth nigh unto me with their mouth, and honoureth me with their lips; but their heart is far from me." Disobedience in deeds of life and behavior nullify the words of one's mouth. Our comportment in life carries more influence than vociferous words from our lips.

> The words, "I know him," in 1 John 2:4 have reference to:
> . . .the pious platitudes, cheap claptrap of the Gnostics, who would bob up in meetings with such explosions. John punctures such bubbles with the sharp addition "and keepeth not." The one who keeps on saying, "I have come to know Him," and keeps on not keeping his commandments is a liar (just like Satan, John 8:44). There is a whip-cracker effect in John's words.[2]

1 John 2:5. But whoso keepeth his word, in him verily is the love of God perfected: hereby know we that we are in him.

The one who keeps on keeping the commandments of Christ pleases the Lord and proves that he is unmistakably of God. The Gnostics by loud talk and loose living denied the Lord even though they boasted that they knew Christ. Surely all of us remember the old adage, "What you do speaks so loud that I cannot hear what you are saying." For example, it is rather difficult for the Sunday School teacher to teach the pupils that Sunday evening service at church is very important if the teacher never comes to the service himself. We teach by example and influence as well as by word.

The one who habitually keeps the Word of Christ is said to have the love of God in him. The word for love is *agapē*. It is the word that speaks of "divine, self-sacrificial love." This love is the love that God has for the whole world, for all mankind (John 3:16), the love shed abroad in our hearts by the Holy Spirit (Rom. 5:5), the love God is as to His very nature (1 John 4:8), the ingredients of which love are found in chapter 13 of 1 Corinthians. It is the love that Christ exhibited at Calvary when He tasted death for every man (Heb. 2:9).

1 John 2:6. He that saith he abideth in him ought himself also so to walk, even as he walked.

The word "abideth" comes from *menō*, meaning "to remain," "to sojourn," "to tarry." It was used to tell of a permanent resident in a city. It was also used of persons abiding at home, which thought, of course, speaks of good fellowship between members of the family at home. The word further speaks of communion, dependence, harmony and friendship.

New Testament examples of the use of the word are found in Matthew 10:11; 26:38; Luke 1:56; 8:27; 19:5; John 1:39 and 40. The reader would do well to look up those verses and meditate upon them for awhile.

To abide in the Lord Jesus, therefore, implies not only *position* but also *relationship*. There are three words that give us three aspects of a believer's life in Christ:

1. *Eimi*, verb of being, refers to the believer's position in Christ, so that the child of God possesses the very life of God. "And this is life eternal, that they might know thee the only true God, and Jesus Christ, whom thou hast sent" (John 17:3).

2. *Menō* refers to the believer's fellowship with and dependence upon the Lord Jesus.

3. *Peripateō*, meaning "to order one's behavior," "to conduct oneself," speaks of the believer's manner of life. It is translated "walk" in the verse.

Let us, then, be resolved to be in the practice of life what we are in the position of grace.

> *1 John 2:7.* Brethren, I write no new commandment unto you, but an old commandment which ye had from the beginning. The old commandment is the word ye have heard from the beginning.

One of the great needs of the hour is not a new revelation, but an earnest and diligent study of the one God has already given to us, with resultant practice of the truth in heart and life.

The word "brethren," used for the first time in the epistle, comes from *adelphos*, derived in turn from *adelphus*, meaning "from the same womb," thus, a fellow believer, a brother in the Lord. The word is frequently used in the Pauline Epistles. One is reminded of Galatians 3:26, "For ye are all the children of God by faith in Christ Jesus." The bond of union of fellow believers is in the Lord Jesus Christ.

All believers are united to the Lord and to one another through the new birth (John 1:13; 3:3, 5-8; 2 Cor. 5:17). Christians are one in Christ because of the nature of salvation (Jude 3), which was planned by the Father, purchased by the Son and perfected by the Holy Spirit, Who regenerates and permanently indwells every child of God (Rom. 5:5). As brethren together in Christ, we need to heed and to practice the revealed truth given to us. "I write unto you" emphasizes the fact that God has already given us His Word. Now we need to commit it to practice each day of our lives through the blessed power of the Holy Spirit.

> *1 John 2:8.* Again, a new commandment I write unto you, which thing is true in him and in you: because the darkness is past, and the true light now shineth.

God has decreed the glorious triumph of truth. Our hearts should be thrilled and encouraged at the ring of the proclamation, "the darkness is past, and the true light now shineth," meaning that:

> The darkness is passing away. The picture is that of the darkness of sin and unbelief as passing by as a parade goes by on the street. All parades have an end. So will end some day the parade of Satan's hosts (KSW, 119).

The true light is "the light of the glorious gospel of Christ" (2 Cor. 4:4).

> *1 John 2:9.* He that saith he is in the light, and hateth his brother, is in darkness even until now.

One dominant characteristic of a mature believer is the exhibition of love for fellow Christians. In 1 John 3:18, we are given instructions on this matter of love for the brethren in the words, "My little children, let us not love in word, neither in tongue; but in deed and in truth."

One of the proofs that we have been with our Lord is that we love the brethren. "Men fall into two classes, those who are in fellowship with God, and therefore walk in light and love, and those who are not in fellowship with God, and therefore walk in darkness and hatred (KSW, 120).

The biting philosophy of the world is, "Dog eat dog." Contrariwise, believers are instructed, "And be ye kind one to another, tenderhearted, forgiving one another, even as God for Christ's sake hath forgiven you" (Eph. 4:32). The glorious difference between the believer's and the world's philosophies is the saving grace of God in the soul. Were it not for the grace of God in our hearts, we too would be heading for a Christless torment in the region of woe.

> *1 John 2:10.* He that loveth his brother abideth in the light, and there is none occasion of stumbling in him.

One leading trait of Christian maturity is a prayerful concern for fellow believers in Christ.

To love one's brother in Christ means to have self-sacrificial love that gives of itself for the happiness and well-being of a fellow Christian. The love of the early Christians impressed the heathen.

As one loves the brethren in the Lord, he abides in the light, a spiritual benediction:

> . . .indicative of his close fellowship with and dependency upon the Lord Jesus, for this supernaturally-produced love in his heart is present in an overflowing quantity only in the life of a believer who habitually is abiding in his Lord. The light here is, of course, the Lord Jesus Himself and all that is written in the Word about Him (KSW, 121).

The words "none occasion of stumbling" are from *skandalon*, "the movable stick or trigger of a trap," "a trap or snare," "any impediment placed in the way and causing one to stumble or fall," "a stumbling block" (KSW, 121). The full meaning of the words is made clearer in the words of another Scripture, "It is good neither to eat flesh, nor to drink wine, nor any thing whereby thy brother stumbleth, or is offended, or is made weak" (Rom. 14:21). Please note the all-inclusive, governing principle of our attitude toward fellow believers, ". . .nor any thing whereby thy brother stumbleth. . . ." Once we have applied this principle, we are ready to give ourselves to the following worthy objective: "Let us therefore follow after the things which make for peace, and things wherewith one may edify another" (Rom. 14:19). Many church problems would be solved at once if we spent half as much time edifying one another as we do causing one another to stumble.

> *1 John 2:11.* But he that hateth his brother is in darkness, and walketh in darkness, and knoweth not whither he goeth, because that darkness hath blinded his eyes.

One who is held by the binding tentacles of hatred is controlled by the awesome power of evil. The devil through nefarious hatred cheats many folk out of the blessing of salvation.

"The first part of the verse repeats verse 9, but adds this vivid touch of the blinding power of darkness. In the Mammoth Cave of Kentucky, the fish of Echo River have eye-sockets, but no eyes."[3]

Engulfed by the terrible power of blinding darkness, the person who constantly comports himself in the sphere of hatred is surely an unsaved person professing Christianity and is a child of the devil.

> *1 John 2:12.* I write unto you, little children, because your sins are forgiven you for his name's sake.

Spiritual power and glory flood our souls as we lay hold of the wonderful message that our sins are forgiven in Christ. Have you ever noticed, during an airplane ride, how thick clouds disappear into nothingness? So the Lord says, "I have blotted out, as a thick cloud, thy transgressions, and, as a cloud, thy sins: return unto me; for I have redeemed thee" (Isa. 44:22).

In 1 John 2:12, the words "I write unto you" mean that God our Father has a special and personal message for us in His Word, calling us His "little children," meaning "little born ones." We are born into the royal family of the redeemed through the blessed power of the Holy Spirit, Who perfects the benefits of the gospel in our hearts (Eph. 1:13), "Who hath delivered us from the power of darkness, and hath translated us into the kingdom of his dear Son" (Col. 1:13), so that we are ". . . partakers of the inheritance of the saints in light" (Col. 1:12b).

Our wonderful redemption in Christ is expressed in the words, ". . . your sins are forgiven you for his name's sake." The words "are forgiven" come from *aphiēmi*, "to send from oneself," "to send away," "to bid go away or depart."

> God's forgiveness includes the putting away of our sins, their guilt, defilement, and penalty, at the Cross. . . . Because of what our Lord was in His Person as very God of very God, God the Father put away our sins, recognizing and accepting the atonement He offered on the cross (KSW, 122, 123).

CHAPTER VI
TRIUMPH OVER THE WORLD

1 John 2:13, 14. I write unto you, fathers, because ye have known him that is from the beginning. I write unto you, young men, because ye have overcome the wicked one. I write unto you, little children, because ye have known the Father.
I have written unto you, fathers, because ye have known him that is from the beginning. I have written unto you, young men, because ye are strong, and the word of God abideth in you, and ye have overcome the wicked one.

Three groups of believers are addressed in these verses:
1. Fathers, mature believers with long and rich experience, who have known Him that is from the beginning, words descriptive of our Lord's eternality (John 1:1).
2. Young men, the younger Christians in contrast to the aging fathers, full of vigor and conflict and victory, who have triumphed over the wicked one, words which tell of Satan's active evil against God and man, but also his defeat in the struggle (John 12:31).
3. Little children, an appellation descriptive of the relationship to God by the new birth (John 3:3, 5), drawing our attention to the basic truth of salvation, which is made a reality in the soul as faith lays hold of the promise of God in the gospel (John 20:31; Heb. 11:6).

Such groups as these newborn ones, young men and older fathers in a local church mean that that church is very much alive, an ideal church, one that is seeing souls saved and other believers growing and maturing in grace, faithfulness and obedience. May the Lord be pleased in these days to give us more such vigorous churches on fire for Christ.

Before we leave these great verses, we need to look a little closer at what is said of the young men in verse 14, namely, ". . . ye are strong. . . ." They are strong because the Word of God abides (is at home) in them. That thought reminds us at once of Psalm 119:11, "Thy word have I hid in mine heart, that I might not sin against thee," a verse sometimes explained and summarized as:

Thy Word—a good thing

Have I hid in mine heart—a good place

That I might not sin against Thee—for a good purpose

We move now to chapter 2, verses 15-17, of 1 John. In these verses there is a discussion of the believer's relationship to the world.

> *1 John 2:15.* Love not the world, neither the things that are in the world. If any man love the world, the love of the Father is not in him.

The problem for believers of all ages has been how to be in the world and yet not of it (John 17:11, 14).

The words "love not the world" are in a construction that means "stop considering the world precious with the result that you love it." One who loves the world is heading fast for frustration and confusion. Everything in the world is in the process of deterioration and decay.

The believer must be ever alert, watchful and diligent in his Christian walk, for the devil's traps and pitfalls infest our pilgrim path. Satan's cunning devices, his deceitful trickery, his wicked hindrances and his fiery darts of hatred are ever in motion to ensnare us and impede our spiritual progress.

The timely, exhortative words of Jeremiah to Baruch are

good for our own time, "And seekest thou great things for thyself? seek them not: for, behold, I will bring evil upon all flesh, saith the LORD . . ." (Jer. 45:5). The good testimony of Demas was ruined because he fell in love with this present evil world. The apostle Paul wrote, "For Demas hath forsaken me, having loved this present world, and is departed unto Thessalonica . . ." (2 Tim. 4:10).

There are disastrous results from a believer's loving the world—the loss of spiritual strength, joy, usefulness and rewards. By loving the world some Christians have missed God's best. The world's blight turns some spiritual giants into powerless dwarfs. Some with chandelier ability have become mere candles by loving the world. Others with ocean liner power have been reduced to tugboat impotency by loving the world. Still others with steam shovel capacity offer to God no more than teaspoon service because the world's allurements steal and sap their best energy.

Let us, then, with hearts aflame with love and true devotion to our Lord, look at the world from a balanced perspective. We are pilgrims traveling through the world to our heavenly Home. There is a spiritual boost for us in the reflection that we are strangers here on our way to the glory world of God. We must not become too attached or too settled down. As pilgrims, we should be always ready to strike our tents at a moment's notice, moving on, out and up to our permanent dwelling place. Our service should be seasoned with the thought that one day we will make our nonstop flight from the burdensome woes of earth to the blessed wonders of Heaven.

Every Bible student ought to have a clear concept of the meaning of the word "world." In the present context it is the word *kosmos,* connoting:

> . . .The sum-total of human life in the ordered world, considered apart from, alienated from, and hostile to God, and of the earthly things which seduce from God (John 7:7; 15:18; 2 Corinthians 7:10; James 4:4). . . it is

the ordered system of which Satan is the head, his fallen angels and demons are his emissaries, and the unsaved of the human race are his subjects, together with those purposes, pursuits, pleasures, practices, and places where God is not wanted. Much in this world-system is religious, cultured, refined, and intellectual. But it is anti-God and anti-Christ (Vincent cited by KSW, 125).

It is impossible to love the world and the Father at the same time (Matt. 6:24).

1 John 2:16. For all that is in the world, the lust of the flesh, and the lust of the eyes, and the pride of life, is not of the Father, but is of the world.

There is here a summary of all possible sins, exemplified in the temptations of Eve (Gen. 3:1-6) and our Lord (Matt. 4:1-11).

The words "the lust of the flesh" refer to "the passionate desire of the craving that comes from the evil nature." The statement "the lust of the eyes" describes "the passionate cravings of the eyes for satisfaction, these cravings finding their source in the evil nature."

Note some descriptions of our eyes in the Bible: opened eyes (Gen. 3:7); that is, eyes opened to nakedness, shame, sin and ruin. ". . . The eyes of the wicked shall fail . . ." (Job 11:20). "Redness of eyes" (Prov. 23:29) speaks of the results of drunkenness. Eyes that see not (Mark 8:18) are descriptive of sinful blindness and the lack of spiritual discernment. "Blessed are the eyes which see" (Luke 10:23) refers to people who have been saved, whose eyes are opened by the Spirit of God to the sunshine of heavenly grace. Ephesians 1:18 speaks of understanding eyes. Second Peter 2:14 refers to "eyes full of adultery." The Psalmist prayed for opened eyes for the study of God's Word and the power to discern spiritual truth: "Open thou mine eyes, that I may behold wondrous things out of thy law" (Ps. 119:18).

The words, "the pride of life," literally "the vainglory of life," have reference to that "insolent and empty assurance which trusts in its own power and resources and shamefully despises and violates divine laws and human rights."[1] "To set one's affection on the things in the world is 'braggart boasting'; for they are not ours, they are transient."[2]

In our love for the Father and rejection of the world, we should remember the real motive for which Christ came into the world: "For ye know the grace of our Lord Jesus Christ, that, though he was rich, yet for your sakes he became poor, that ye through his poverty might be rich" (2 Cor. 8:9). Our blessed Lord gave up a throne for a tree. He gave up the riches of Heaven for the rags of earth. Our Savior gave up the glory of Heaven for the gory things of earth. What powerful bands of devotion should bind us to our main task of love and service to our Lord during these troublesome times! We should ever be telling the story of salvation, ever serving our Lord since He has done so much for us—dying for our sins that we might live unto God through the completed, redemptive work at Calvary.

> *1 John 2:17.* And the world passeth away, and the lust thereof: but he that doeth the will of God abideth for ever.

What a striking contrast: the world passes away, but he that does the will of God abides forever. The world is headed up by Satan and is bound for judgment: "Because he hath appointed a day, in the which he will judge the world in righteousness by that man whom he hath ordained; whereof he hath given assurance unto all men, in that he hath raised him from the dead" (Acts 17:31).

The nations of people are talking about escape, hoping for and seeking a solution to earth's baffling difficulties. But, to be sure, there is no escape except through Jesus Christ Who gives salvation to the soul, as well as blessing and liberty to our lives now. Believers are admonished to, "Stand fast

therefore in the liberty wherewith Christ hath made us free
. . ." (Gal. 5:1). Thank God for the free liberty in Christ—that
glorious liberty which frees us from sin, and, as well, liber-
ates us from the involvements of this world so that we can
serve our God. Yes, Christ is the answer for man's ills, for
time and eternity. God has made a way through the blood of
the Lord Jesus Christ. "If the Son therefore shall make you
free, ye shall be free indeed" (John 8:36).

The words "passeth away" in 1 John 2:17 mean "to pass
alongside," "to pass by." The god of this world, Satan, offers
false hopes and escape. Even the actual observer will notice
that earthly things are passing away. There is no sure foundation here. Our souls cannot find permanent rest in the
restless things of earth.

> The world is being caused to pass by. That is, God is
> causing the world to come to its end. It is being caused
> to pass by in a vain (futile) show, this parade of the
> world (KSW, 128).

Believers must not ever forget that the world's gold and
glitter is much like a treacherous octopus, ever thrusting out
its probing tentacles, seeking to allure and entrap the child
of God in its evil philosophy. "Beware lest any man spoil you
through philosophy and vain deceit, after the tradition of
men, after the rudiments of the world, and not after Christ"
(Col. 2:8).

The verse concludes with a shout of victory, sounding out
the provisions for blessed triumph over the world's entangle-
ments, "The one who keeps on habitually doing the will of
God abides for ever!"

CHAPTER VII
CONFIDENCE AT HIS COMING

This chapter will complete the second general division of the epistle, **fellowship with God in light** (1 John 1:5—2:28). Let us consider the believer's blessed relationship to God by grace contrasted with the unbeliever's plight of inevitable judgment (1 John 2:18-28).

> *1 John 2:18, 19.* Little children, it is the last time: and as ye have heard that antichrist shall come, even now are there many antichrists; whereby we know that it is the last time.
> They went out from us, but they were not of us: for if they had been of us, they would no doubt have continued with us: but they went out, that they might be made manifest that they were not all of us.

Let us never forget that the Word of God is our source book of divine knowledge, Heaven's wisdom and spiritual understanding. God has given us His Word so that we might know what to expect in the last time.

How can we be sure of God's blessing upon our lives during the days ahead? Let us be obedient, standing for the truth of God's Word, living a life of testimony before the world to the praise of our God (Ps. 90:12; Matt. 5:16).

The Word teaches us that the Antichrist will come. In John's day there were already many antichrists in the world, just as there are now. The antichrists of John's time and the present time are forerunners of the coming one who will embody all the wickedness of his predecessors.

All false professors of Christ prove by action and deed that they are not of God by committing the evil act of apostasy. Antichrists are those who lift themselves up "instead of Christ." They are ungodly forerunners of the coming Antichrist of the tribulation time, about whom the Scriptures speak in 2 Thessalonians 2:3 and 4:

> . . . And that man of sin be revealed, the son of perdition;
>
> Who opposeth and exalteth himself above all that is called God, or that is worshipped; so that he as God sitteth in the temple of God, shewing himself that he is God.

Antichrist's doom and destiny are cited in Revelation 19:20. Contextually the Gnostics were antichrists. Modernists and liberals of varying shades are antichrists since they have denied the faith. The pope of Rome by avowed claim is an antichrist, asserting himself to be the vicar ("instead of") of God on earth. The Bible student should remember that the word "anti" means more than "against." The basic meaning of the word is "instead of."

The term "last time" is used twice in 1 John 2:18. The same thought appears elsewhere and is translated as follows: 1 Timothy 4:1, "latter times"; 2 Timothy 3:1, "last days"; Hebrews 1:2, "last days"; 1 Peter 1:20, "last times."

Many present-day cultists have used the phrase "last time" to engage in senseless date-setting. Such speculation has resulted in the embracing of heresies.

Without getting into exhaustive involvement, one could say that the term "last time," and its equivalents, refers to the period from before Pentecost until Christ's return (Joel 2:28-32 and Acts 2:15-21).

According to the Word, then, this present age is to be characterized by the infestation of multiple antichrists, namely, those religions, systems and individuals who put themselves up "in the place of" Christ.

The many antichrists of John's time proved that they were not of God by their deeds and behavior.

> These false teachers (antichrists) went out from the true believers in the sense that they departed doctrinally from the position of the Church as to the Person of the Lord Jesus, a position which they had held only in an intellectual way. It was a mental assent to the doctrines concerning, not a heart acceptance of, the Person of Christ.

> In the words "They were not of us," we have the ablative of source. That is, the antichrists did not have their source in the Mystical Body of Christ composed only of true believers. They were merely members of the visible, organized church on earth. They did not partake of the divine life animating the members of the Body of Christ, made up of true believers. All of which means that an apostate is an unsaved person who has mentally subscribed to the doctrines . . . while still remaining within the organization of the visible church and posing as a Christian (KSW, 131).

> *1 John 2:20, 21.* But ye have an unction from the Holy One, and ye know all things.
> I have not written unto you because ye know not the truth, but because ye know it, and that no lie is of the truth.

Believers are taught of the Holy Spirit to know the truth and to detect error.

The term "unction" renders *chrisma.*

> The word refers to that with which the anointing is performed, the unguent or ointment. Here it refers to the Holy Spirit with whom the believer is anointed. . . . The anointing with the Holy Spirit refers to the act of

> God the Father ... sending the Spirit in answer to the prayer of God the Son to take up His permanent residence in the believer....This anointing is never repeated (KSW, 132).

The Holy Spirit is the great Teacher Whose illuminating ministry enables believers to understand the Word of God. A preacher prayed, "Oh, God, illuminate Thy Word tonight!" But it is the messenger, not the Word, that needs illumination. As a result of the indwelling of the Holy Spirit, the saints are given the ability to know God's truth.

> The particular word for "know" here is not *ginoskō*, "to know by experience," but *oida*, "to know absolutely and finally." The antichrists, being unsaved and thus devoid of the Holy Spirit, do not have that ability. This ability to know the truth gives the saints the ability also to detect error (KSW, 133).

> *1 John 2:22, 23.* Who is a liar but he that denieth that Jesus is the Christ? He is antichrist, that denieth the Father and the Son.
> Whosoever denieth the Son, the same hath not the Father: [but] he that acknowledgeth the Son hath the Father also.

Verse 22 describes antichrists (ancient Gnostics, modern liberals) as liars because they deny the Son and the Father.

The definite article appears before the word "liar" in the Greek text—"Who is *the* liar?"

> The words are aimed at the heresy of Cerinthus, a man of Jewish descent and educated at Alexandria. He denied the miraculous conception of Jesus, and taught that, after His baptism, the Christ descended upon Him in the form of a dove, and that He then announced the unknown Father and wrought miracles; but that, towards the end of His ministry, the Christ departed again from Jesus, and Jesus suffered and rose from

the dead, while the Christ remained impassible (incapable of suffering) as a spiritual being.[1]

Involved in the denial of Jesus Christ is the rejection of His deity, humanity and vicarious atonement. The gnostic, antichristian error, therefore, was the denial that the:

> ... Person called Jesus was neither God nor man, and that on the Cross He did not offer atonement for sin. Present-day Modernism denies the deity of Jesus of Nazareth and the substitutionary atonement He offered on the Cross, while subscribing to His humanity. Modernism is branded here by John as "the liar" (KSW, 135).

A denial of the Son is equal to a denial of the Father since the Father is manifested and interpreted in the Son (John 1:18; 14:9).

> *1 John 2:24-26.* Let that therefore abide in you, which ye have heard from the beginning. If that which ye have heard from the beginning shall remain in you, ye also shall continue in the Son, and in the Father.
> And this is the promise that he hath promised us, even eternal life.
> These things have I written unto you concerning them that seduce you.

In striking contrast to the miserable plight of the antichristian Gnostics, those who are true believers, children of God, saved by the grace of God, persist in the truth of the gospel and hence are everlastingly secure within the keeping power of God (1 Pet. 1:5).

The words, "he hath promised us ... eternal life," bring ringing assurance to our souls. What wonderful words of everlasting joy that in Christ we now have eternal life. God the Father is the Promiser and His promises are made in Christ (2 Cor. 1:20).

The keeping power of God is not a fictitious dream but a

sure reality. The security of the believer is a blessed fact of the gospel, grounded in the infallible promises of God. Let us note that:

> This comforting promise of eternal life is anchored in God's sovereign will, beyond the blow of time's deterioration and decay. It is settled in a holy God and cannot be damaged by sin's destructive power. It is enthroned in an omnipotent God who will see to its coming to pass. It is founded, forever, in an omniscient God, beyond the frustration of man, angel, demon or devil. In short, this promise is unfailing because God Himself stands back of it, guaranteeing that its fulfillment cannot be jeopardized by any creature in heaven, on earth, or under the earth—not by angel above, man on earth, or demon under the earth.[2]

> *1 John 2:27*. But the anointing which ye have received of him abideth in you, and ye need not that any man teach you: but as the same anointing teacheth you of all things, and is truth, and is no lie, and even as it hath taught you, ye shall abide in him.

It is a wonderful Biblical truth to know that believers are permanently indwelt by the Holy Spirit (Rom. 5:5). The Holy Spirit guides, teaches, comforts, strengthens and takes the things of Christ and shows them unto us, always encouraging us in the things of the Lord (John 14:26; 16:13, 14).

The children of God are described as those who know. The words, "and ye know all things," have been translated, "and you all know" or "all you all know" that they will not be led astray since they have received the enlightening grace of the Holy Spirit, "Which he shed on us abundantly (richly) through Jesus Christ our Saviour" (Titus 3:6).

> *1 John 2:28*. And now, little children, abide in him; that when he shall appear, we may have confidence, and not be ashamed before him at his coming.

The way to victorious Christian living is to appropriate the abundant provisions God has provided for holy living in His Word, that we may have confidence before our Lord at His coming at the Rapture of the Church.

First Thessalonians 4:12 and 5:22 admonish, "That ye may walk honestly toward them that are without, and that ye may have lack of nothing." "Abstain from all appearance of evil." There is a tremendous need today among God's people for an emphasis upon holy living, to become in life and deed what we are already in heart and soul by God's grace, to practice on the outside what God has already made us on the inside, so that our standing in Christ will equal our state, that we may receive a full reward at His coming.

CHAPTER VIII
SHOWING THAT WE BELONG TO GOD

The third general division of 1 John is **fellowship with God in righteousness** (1 John 2:29—4:6).

For our meditation, we will consider the righteousness and love of God in the heart manifested in life, word and deed.

> *1 John 2:29.* If ye know that he is righteous, ye know that every one that doeth righteousness is born of him.

The first "know" translates *eidēte,* from *oida,* meaning "to know absolutely." The second "know" is from another word, *ginoskō,* "to know experientially." Our salvation, to be sure, is an unmistakable, certain living relationship with God, grounded forever in His indestructible counsels. This living faith of heart and soul expresses itself in acts and deeds of obedience to our Lord.

The term "born" is in a construction that speaks of a past completed action having present results, literally, "having been born with the present result that you are a child of God by birth." The word "born" further speaks of the truth that the relationship between God and the believer as Father and child is a permanent one, making the security of the believer a satisfying reality. This glorious truth calls to our minds the words of Isaiah 51:6:

> Lift up your eyes to the heavens, and look upon the
> earth beneath: for the heavens shall vanish away like
> smoke, and the earth shall wax old like a garment, and
> they that dwell therein shall die in like manner: but my
> salvation shall be for ever, and my righteousness shall
> not be abolished.

"Doeth" in 1 John 2:29 comes from the present tense participle of *poieō*, which construction speaks of continuous action. This means that the habitual doing of God's will is in view here.

> The habitual actions of a person are an index to his
> character. The habitual actions of righteousness, God's
> righteousness here as produced by the Holy Spirit (the
> definite article stands before the word "righteousness"
> in the Greek text, marking this out as a particular
> righteousness) is an indication of regeneration (KSW,
> 140, 141).

> *1 John 3:1.* Behold, what manner of love the Father
> hath bestowed upon us, that we should be called the
> sons of God: therefore the world knoweth us not, be-
> cause it knew him not.

This is one of the great verses in the Bible on the love of God. The Father is presented in the Bible as the One Who elects, loves and bestows; God the Son is the One Who suffers, redeems and upholds; God the Holy Spirit is the One Who regenerates, energizes and sanctifies. As to our salvation, God the Father planned it, God the Son purchased it and God the Holy Spirit perfects it in the heart of the believer.

How amazing it is that we, wretched, unworthy sinners, should be the recipients of God's wonderful love, so that we are called the sons of God.

The word for love is *agapē*, the divine, self-sacrificial love that God is as to His nature (1 John 4:8), that He has for the world (John 3:16), that is shed abroad in our hearts by the Holy Spirit (Rom. 5:5) and for which the ingredients are found in 1 Corinthians 13. What a tremendous cause for boundless praise that the love of God avails for the eternal salvation of our souls.

The words, "what manner of," mean "from what country, race or tribe." It could also be rendered "from what realm? What unearthly love. How other-worldly" (Smith cited by KSW, 142). This means that:

> the love of God is foreign to the human race. It is not found naturally in humanity. When it exists there, it is in a saved individual, and by reason of the ministry of the Holy Spirit (KSW, 142).

Because we now and forever belong to the Lord, the world, that is, the people of the world system of evil headed up by Satan (1 John 2:15-17), does not know us in the sense of appreciation and understanding.

> Since the people of the world have nothing in common with the children of God, they have no fellowship with them, and therefore have no intelligent appreciation and understanding of them. The foreign kind of love produced in us by the Holy Spirit constitutes us a foreign kind of person to the people of this world, and since they do not understand foreigners, people of a different race from themselves, they simply do not understand Christians. Children of God could just as well have come to earth from a strange planet so far as the people of the world are concerned. They are strangers to them (KSW, 143).

> *1 John 3:2.* Beloved, now are we the sons of God, and it doth not yet appear what we shall be: but we know that, when he shall appear, we shall be like him; for we shall see him as he is.

The believer right now possesses a know-so salvation, as

well as the assurance of a glorious destiny in being con-
formed to the likeness of the Lord Jesus.

> The two thoughts of the present and future condition
> of God's children are placed side by side with the sim-
> ple copula, and, as parts of one thought. Christian con-
> dition, now and eternally, centers in the fact of being
> children of God. In that fact lies the germ of all the
> possibilities of eternal life.[1]

We are now sons of God by grace through faith. We have a
blessed filial relationship with God for time and eternity, a
result of appropriating the provisions God has made for our
souls in the vicarious atonement of His Son, the Lord Jesus.
Salvation of the soul becomes a joyful reality as Christ is
received into the heart. The fact that God is our Father by
faith is an unshakable truth.

Need we to remind ourselves that one out of every twenty-
five verses of the New Testament speaks of our Lord's second coming? When He comes, we shall be like Him. All that
is involved in being like Him we cannot fully know this side
of eternity. We do know, however, that being like Him and
seeing Him as He is will fulfill our fondest dreams of being
made perfect like Him. The provisions for complete moral
perfection are supplied by the grace of God. Job of old had
this same throbbing hope in his soul, expressed in the words:

> For I know that my redeemer liveth, and that he shall
> stand at the latter day upon the earth:
> And though after my skin worms destroy this body, yet
> in my flesh shall I see God:
> Whom I shall see for myself, and mine eyes shall be-
> hold, and not another; though my reins be consumed
> within me (Job 19:25-27).

> *1 John 3:3.* And every man that hath this hope in him
> purifieth himself, even as he is pure.

The truth of the second coming of our Lord has potent

practical effects for purity of life as no other doctrine in the Scriptures.

The words "every man that hath" are a characteristic form of expression with John. Such expressions usually contain a reference to some who had questioned the application of a general principle to particular cases. Here it applies to some individuals who had denied the practical obligation to moral purity involved in their hope.

The term "hope" does not mean "wishful thinking" or something that might fail of fulfillment. Rather, it refers to that which we know shall come to pass in accordance with the promise of God (Acts 1:9-11). Therefore we should live in constant watchfulness for the premillennial, prerapture return of our blessed Savior. The word "hope" is used in Romans 15:12, "in him shall the Gentiles [hope]"; and in 1 Timothy 4:10, "We [hope] in the living God."

Living in the attitude of the expected fulfillment of our Lord's coming will be a strong incentive for us to constantly keep our spiritual house in order so that we will not be ashamed before Him at His coming. First Thessalonians 1:10 exhorts us on this wise, "And to wait for his Son from heaven, whom he raised from the dead, even Jesus, which delivered us from the wrath to come." The word "wait" is from *anamenein*, "to wait for one with added notion of patience and trust." The word is used in the present tense and speaks of daily watchfulness and expectation. Gross wickedness and licentious evil easily become the way of those who cease to look for the Lord Jesus' return.

> *1 John 3:4.* Whosoever committeth sin transgresseth also the law: for sin is the transgression of the law.

John shows the incompatibility of being a child of God and yet continuing in sin.

> "Committeth" is from *poieō*, "to do." Rev., better, *every one that doeth sin.* The phrase *to do sin* regards sin as something actually realized in its completeness.

> He that *does sin* realizes in action *the* sin (note the arti-
> cle the), that which includes and represents the com-
> plete ideal of sin. Compare do *righteousness,* ii.29.[2]

"Transgresseth the law" is literally "doeth lawlessness."
Sin and lawlessness are identical. The present tense construction means the habit of doing sin. The reference is to an
unsaved person who claims to know God but still lives constantly in sin. The contextual reference has in mind the
Gnostic who with a loud voice claimed to know God but who
denied the Lord by disobedient deeds. Our Lord said to the
Pharisees, ". . . Most assuredly I am saying to you, everyone
who habitually commits sin is a slave of sin" (John 8:34,
Wuest's translation). Compare also Matthew 7:23, "And then
will I profess unto them, I never knew you: depart from me,
ye that work [constantly] iniquity."

> *1 John 3:5.* And ye know that he was manifested to take
> away our sins; and in him is no sin.

God has made every provision for our salvation. The Lord
Jesus Christ is a satisfying, suitable, all-sufficient Savior.
"He was manifested" translates the Greek word *ephane-
rothē* and refers to Christ's appearing in the flesh as God incarnate (John 1:14; 1 Tim. 3:16), "the fulness of the Godhead
bodily" (Col. 2:9), the virgin-born Son of God (Matt. 1:23; Gal.
4:4), the sinless Savior Who died for our sins upon the cross,
thereby liquidating in full our sin-debt, enabling God to "be
just, and the justifier of him which believeth in Jesus" (Rom.
3:26).
The words "and in him is no sin" (1 John 3:5) emphasize
the moral perfection of our Lord. In every way He is fully
qualified to be our Savior.

> Jesus is pure. He had no sin. He did no sin. No guile
> was found in His mouth. The thoughts of His mind, the
> motives of His heart, and the deeds of His life were not
> tainted by the stigma of iniquity. Jesus, the only Sav-

ior, was untouched by sin's vitiating germs. No horrible wrong ever blackened His unblemished life.[3]

1 John 3:6. Whosoever abideth in him sinneth not: whosoever sinneth hath not seen him, neither known him.

The words "abideth" and "sinneth" are used here to designate a certain class of individual. Character is shown by one's habitual actions, not the extraordinary ones. The tense of the verbs is present, the kind of action, continuous, habitual. Thus, . . . "every one who habitually is sinning," [is] an unsaved person. A Christian as a habit of life is abiding in fellowship with the Lord Jesus. Sin may at times enter his life. But sin is the exception, not the rule. The unsaved person as a habit of life sins continually. "Sinneth" is present in tense, continuous action being indicated. The person who is abiding in Christ is not habitually sinning. The child of God as a habit of life, does righteousness, and sin is not a habit with him. John is not teaching sinless perfection here. John does not teach that believers do not sin, but is speaking of a character, a habit. Throughout the Epistle, he deals with the ideal reality of life in God, in which the love of God and sin exclude each other as light and darkness. He does not deny that a Christian sins at times. Indeed he admits the possibility of sin in the Christian's life in 1:9, and forbids sin in 2:1. What John denies here is that a Christian sins habitually. He denies that the life of a Christian is wholly turned towards sin as is that of the unsaved person (KSW, 147, 148).

The person who constantly lives a life of habitual sin demonstrates conclusively that he is not of God, is not saved. "The habit of sin is proof that one has not the vision or the knowledge of Christ."[4]

CHAPTER IX
CHILDREN OF THE LIGHT, STANDING FOR THE RIGHT

Since he has God's love in his heart, the believer constantly practices righteousness in love for God and for the children of God while overtly abhorring that which is of the devil (1 John 3:7-14).

> *1 John 3:7.* Little children, let no man deceive you: he that doeth righteousness is righteous, even as he is righteous.

This verse is almost the same as 2:29, except here the oft-used term of endearment, "little children," meaning "little born ones," is added, emphasizing once again the truth that only those born of God according to the unchangeable terms of the gospel really belong to God. Here also is the added exhortation, "let no man deceive you," literally, "stop allowing anyone to be leading you astray."

One's pious and loud talk is no guarantee that he belongs to God. Mouthing words does not adequately substitute for heart possession. The Gnostics claimed to know God but in words they denied Him. Scripture forbids us to judge before the time, but we can Scripturally inspect fruit. Let us set our compass, then, by the Word of God, for therein we are told: "Beware of false prophets, which come to you in sheep's clothing, but inwardly they are ravening wolves. Ye shall know [fully recognize] them by their fruits. . ." (Matt. 7:15,

16). Modernists employ Scriptural terminology to deceive the unwary just as the devil misused Scripture in the temptation of our Lord (cf. Matthew 4:1-11 with Psalm 91).

> *1 John 3:8-10.* He that committeth sin is of the devil; for the devil sinneth from the beginning. For this purpose the Son of God was manifested, that he might destroy the works of the devil.
> Whosoever is born of God doth not commit sin; for his seed remaineth in him: and he cannot sin, because he is born of God.
> In this the children of God are manifest, and the children of the devil: whosoever doeth not righteousness is not of God, neither he that loveth not his brother.

Let us concentrate on the real meaning of these verses which are so often "eisegeted" instead of "exegeted," the former method meaning to read something into the text which is not there and the latter term meaning to lift out of the text what is there.

False doctrine, cults and isms always thrive on sheer ignorance of what the Word teaches. Our Lord said to the Sadducees, "Ye do err, not knowing the scriptures . . ." (Matt. 22:29).

Some see in these verses sinless perfection, the uprooting of the old Adamic nature, so that one is able to live above sin and not sin anymore in this life. Others say that if a believer fails in even one instance he will fall from grace, or lose his salvation, and will have to be saved all over again or he will miss Heaven.

The informed Bible student knows that neither of the above-mentioned teachings is found in these verses. However, if there is an earnest brother who has difficulty here, let him know that such difficulty can be quickly resolved by noting the kind of action in the verb tense employed. The present tense is used, which speaks of continuous action, habitual practice. The following expanded translation of these verses will clear up for us any misunderstanding and set before us a delectable banquet of good spiritual eating on the table of sound exegesis:

> The one who is habitually committing sin is out of the devil as a source, because from the beginning the devil has been sinning. For this purpose there was manifested the Son of God, in order that He might bring to naught the works of the devil. Everyone who has been born out of God with the present result that he is a born-one of God does not habitually commmit sin because His seed remains in him. And he is not able to habitually sin, because out of God he has been born with the present result that he is a born-one of God. In this is apparent the born-ones of God and the born-ones of the devil. Every one who is not habitually doing righteousness is not of God, also the one who is not habitually loving his brother (Christian) with a divine and self-sacrificial love.[1]

> *1 John 3:11.* For this is the message that ye heard from the beginning, that we should love one another.

All believers are born of God; hence, they are the blessed recipients of God's nature (2 Pet. 1:4) and God's life (John 17:3). Therefore, it is a natural response for us to love one another, expressing outwardly the inwrought grace of God operative in the salvation of our souls. Our salvation is in its very nature life-changing and habit-altering, having radical impact upon the moral base of our personalities, transforming scorn into concern, hate into love and selfishness into sharing. The Holy Spirit brings into our hearts the love of God so that we can love one another with warmest regard, deepest kindness and most gentle tenderness. It was said of the early Christians, "Behold, how they love one another." The Ephesians, and us as well, were admonished:

Let all bitterness, and wrath, and anger, and clamour, and evil speaking, be put away from you, with all malice:
And be ye kind one to another, tenderhearted, forgiving one another, even as God for Christ's sake hath forgiven you (Eph. 4:31, 32).

Loving one another with a pure heart fervently in the Lord makes for good understanding among the brethren. Being able to get along with one another is an evidence of Christian maturity. Confusion and frustration abound in a church where hot heads and cold hearts sit in the driver's seat. Conversely, happy is that church and blessed are those people where cool heads and warm hearts set the pace.

1 John 3:12. Not as Cain, who was of that wicked one, and slew his brother. And wherefore slew he him? Because his own works were evil, and his brother's righteous.

The words "wicked" and "evil" are from the same strong word for evil used to refer to Satan and his malicious followers. The word is *ponēros*, "bad," "of a bad nature or condition." It describes the wicked activity of Satan in an effort to drag as many as possible down to destruction with him. Our word "pernicious" is a good translation of it.

Cain is a long-standing example of hatred and bloodshed. With the devil in his heart, anger in his eyes and murder throbbing in his soul, he laid hold of Abel while they were in the field together (Gen. 4:8). With a sharp instrument of death, Cain cut his brother's throat (Greek word for "slew" means "to slit the throat"). Abel's blood soaked the earth about him and he fell down dead. The daring, glaring motive of murderous Cain was simply "because his own works were evil, and his brother's righteous." Cain's dastardly deed fired the first shot of the long battle between ancient modernism and fundamentalism, and back of that shot of Cain's was the devil, the archcorrupter of sound doctrine. A modernist is one who rejects salvation by blood and substitutes human works for the grace of God. Cain was the first modernist. He rejected God's Word and Way since he had been taught by Adam that a blood sacrifice is necessary in order to be acceptable before God. God had taught Adam the truth of salvation by blood (cf. Genesis 3:7 with 3:21).

A fundamentalist believes in salvation by blood through the grace of God. Abel for all practical purposes was the progenitor of fundamentalism. Under test he had offered an acceptable blood sacrifice. He would not sell out his convictions for expedient compromise even though it meant losing his life. His separatist stand for the truth has this approbation from God, "By faith Abel offered unto God a more excellent sacrifice than Cain, by which he obtained witness that he was righteous, God testifying of his gifts: and by it he being dead yet speaketh" (Heb. 11:4). In these days of cheap compromise and sinful expediency, may God grant us grace to stand for the right and against the wrong.

> *1 John 3:13.* Marvel not, my brethren, if the world hate you.

Let no one think for a moment that this world's opposition to the gospel has changed. The world is opposed to God and to the people of God—whoever and wherever they are. Our Lord said:

> If the world hate you, ye know that it hated me before it hated you.
> If ye were of the world, the world would love his own: but because ye are not of the world, but I have chosen you out of the world, therefore the world hateth you (John 15:18, 19).

If we are not of the world and not like the world, it will cost us to remain true to God. We will have to pay a price for our stand—but it will be worth it on that day when we stand before our Lord. One reason many so-called believers get along so nicely with the world is because they are so much like it. I recall the terrific cost of refusing to be like the world in the army during World War II. The devilish tirades and the jeering scorn would have sunk me in the waters of despair but for the sustaining grace of God. Yes, if you take a stand against the world, the flesh and the devil it will cost you a dear price. Quit compromising and let the devil have it with both barrels and he will retaliate in a furious rage! Be a fence-straddling, positive-only fellow and everyone will just love you and say, "Oh, he is such a nice little guy." But battle for the truth and the right and war against the wrong and people will say, "Well, he is just another all-negative, fundamental dunce." Now, don't you think that's a little misleading? Do the enemies of the cross have a right to equate a Bible-believing, separatist fundamentalist with a senseless nincompoop whose mental resources are suffering from a gross lack of intelligence? No, but they will say such things nevertheless. So, brother, you still better take your stand in these days and fight the good fight of faith! The Lord will give grace, glory and the victory, for the battle is the Lord's. "Finally, my brethren, be strong in the Lord, and in the power of his might" (Eph. 6:10).

CHAPTER X
ETERNAL LIFE,
THE MOST PRICELESS GIFT

Children of God, blessed recipients of the ineffable gift of eternal life, are exhorted to live out this life in word and deed in association and relationship with other believers (1 John 3:15-24).

> *1 John 3:15.* Whosoever hateth his brother is a murderer: and ye know that no murderer hath eternal life abiding in him.

The terrible word "hateth" is from *miseō,* "to hate," "to pursue with hatred," "to detest." One who bottles up the black poisonous liquid of hate in his heart to extract it upon whom he will proves by such awful deed that he does not have God in his soul and is a total stranger to God's saving grace. Like the ancient Gnostic, he is an empty professor without possession. Hate is of the devil, like the indescribable blackness of hell. Everyone who hates is a potential murderer. The Word of God solemnly speaks, ". . . and ye [believers] know that no murderer hath eternal life abiding in him."

> *1 John 3:16.* Hereby perceive we the love of God, because he laid down his life for us: and we ought to lay down our lives for the brethren.

The term "perceived" is from:

a word which speaks of knowledge gained by experience. The saints have experienced the love of God in that He laid down His life for them, and in that they have become the recipients of salvation. This knowledge is a permanent possession (KSW, 153).

The wonderfully glorious love of God is demonstrated in that the Lord Jesus Christ laid down His life for us. "Life" is *psuchē*, "soul," meaning that:

> Our Lord's death on the cross involved not only His physical death, but abandonment from God because of human sin laid on Him. It was this that touched His soul and caused Him to cry out, "My God, My God, why hast thou forsaken me? (KSW, 154).

In focusing our attention here upon the substitutionary death of our Lord for us, we need also at this time to refresh our spirits by remembering the literal, bodily, physical resurrection of our Lord. The resurrection of the Lord Jesus was a mighty triumph over the forces of death, the devil and hell. He came forth victoriously from the sealed sepulchre as the almighty Conqueror of the ages, giving us hope in the face of death, loosing us with the hands of redemption from the cords of sin and shame. What pure love God had for us, poor, wretched, miserable sinners apart from His grace. Think of the words again, "the love of God"! Those words defy description by man or angel. Human searching cannot ever fully explore the vast treasures of God's amazing love. God has revealed His love to us. Otherwise we could not believe it. Reflect for awhile upon the all-inclusive scope of God's love for us in our need:

1. A Savior to save us from our sins
2. Joy and peace in our hearts today
3. A home in Heaven forever
4. Redemption of the soul and spirit now and glorification of the body at His coming.

Can we measure the love of God? Never! No more than we

could put Niagara Falls in a gallon bucket, or the Pacific Ocean in a teaspoon, or the mighty Amazon in a water pipe! This love of God should so flood our souls that "we ought to lay down our lives for the brethren." "Ought" is *opheilō*, speaking of moral obligation. "Lives" again is *psuchē*, "soul."

> The ego must be crucified. Self must be denied for the benefit of one's brother. It must be kept in mind that our Lord's death had atoning value, whereas our laying down our lives in glad service to our fellow man does not (KSW, 154).

> *1 John 3:17-19.* But whoso hath this world's good, and seeth his brother have need, and shutteth up his bowels of compassion from him, how dwelleth the love of God in him?
> My little children, let us not love in word, neither in tongue; but in deed and in truth.
> And hereby we know that we are of the truth, and shall assure our hearts before him.

A definition of a New Testament local church is a church composed of born-again, baptized believers, banded together in voluntary fellowship, meeting together regularly for worship, for the purpose of preaching the gospel, practicing the keeping of the ordinances (of which there are just two, baptism and the Lord's Supper), carrying out the duties of the Great Commission, given to the church by the Head of the church, the Lord Jesus, which duties involve, among other things, evangelism and missions. An understanding of this definition tells us that Christians are in fellowship with one another; there is a togetherness. Such a relationship is best kept when we understand one another, a mark of spiritual maturity. Sharing material means as the need may arise helps also to bind us together. Many churches have a Fellowship Fund to help those in need. Furthermore, we need to love each other so we will be concerned about one another, praying for our brethren in the Lord, loving not in word and tongue but in deed and in truth. If we practice these things, we "shall assure our hearts before him" in growth and grace.

> *1 John 3:20, 21.* For if our heart condemn us, God is greater than our heart, and knoweth all things.
> Beloved, if our heart condemn us not, then have we confidence toward God.

The words, "If our heart condemn us not," do not claim sinless perfection, but represent the heart attitude of a saint that so far as he knows has no unconfessed sin in his life, has nothing between himself and the Lord Jesus, a saint who is yielded habitually to the Holy Spirit and living in close fellowship with his Lord.

"Confidence" is parresia, "freedom in speaking," "unreservedness in speech," "free and fearless confidence," "cheerful courage," "boldness," "assurance." "Toward" is *pros*, "facing," "toward," thus, "face to face" with God, "facing" God. The article appears before "God" here, thus referring the word "God" to God the Father (KSW, 156).

> *1 John 3:22.* And whatsoever we ask, we receive of him, because we keep his commandments, and do those things that are pleasing in his sight.

Blessed is the pathway of the yielded, obedient believer since God has promised, ". . . no good thing will he withhold from them that walk uprightly" (Ps. 84:11). Living in a manner pleasing to the Lord makes for spiritual growth and progress. King Saul's rapid and miserable downfall came about through disobedience. Scripture reminds us:

> And Samuel said, Hath the LORD as great delight in burnt offerings and sacrifices, as in obeying the voice of the LORD? Behold, to obey is better than sacrifice,

and to hearken than the fat of rams" (1 Sam. 15:22).

"Ask" is *aiteō*, "to ask for," and in the present subjunctive, speaking of continuous action. It is, "whatever we keep on asking for," speaking of repeated and continuous praying, day after day. "The prerequisites for answered prayer are an uncondemning heart, the habitual keeping of God's commandments, and the habitual doing of those things which please Him (KSW, 157).

1 John 3:23, 24. And this is his commandment, That we should believe on the name of his Son Jesus Christ, and love one another, as he gave us commandment. And he that keepeth his commandments dwelleth in him, and he in him. And hereby we know that he abideth in us, by the Spirit which he hath given us.

To be sure, salvation is a free, unmerited gift, bestowed freely, abundantly and permanently upon the one who believes in the Lord Jesus Christ as Savior. To believe on Christ is to commit one's soul to Him, relying upon Him completely for salvation from sin, redemption from ruin, justification from guilt and deliverance from spiritual death. Trusting in the Savior is described in Scripture as *coming* to Christ (Matt. 11:28); *receiving* Him (John 1:12); *hearing* the Word of God (John 5:24); *taking* the water of life freely (Rev. 22:17).

When one believes in the Lord Jesus Christ for soul salvation, God performs a mighty miraculous work of redeeming grace in the heart, making that person a child of God, with a home in Heaven. At the same moment, the Holy Spirit comes (Rom. 5:5) to take up His permanent dwelling place in the believer, leading, teaching and guiding him throughout life, making him to rejoice with daily joy and abounding victory all his life through.

CHAPTER XI
FOR DOCTRINAL GOOD HEALTH—BEWARE OF FALSE PROPHETS

First John 4:1-6 will complete the third division of John's epistle, **fellowship with God in righteousness** (1 John 2:29—4:6).

> *1 John 4:1.* Beloved, believe not every spirit, but try the spirits whether they are of God: because many false prophets are gone out into the world.

"Beloved" is *agapetoi,* a tender term of endearment used also in verses 7 and 11 of this chapter. It means "divinely-loved ones," speaking of our unique relationship to God by His grace. This tender form of address awakens our hearts immediately to receive the solemn warning concerning false prophets, nefarious corrupters of the Word of God.

The words "believe not" are in a construction that forbids the continuation of an action already in progress. It means therefore, "Stop believing," that is, "Stop believing every spirit." We are not to lend our ears or to give of our time or attention to heretics. Some believers, however, in John's time were being carried away with the errors of the Gnostics (Wuest, 159). "Credulity means gullibility and some believers fall easy victims to the latest fads in spiritualistic humbuggery."[1] A strong case in point is the myriads of believers who have gone wildly after the current sweeping rampage of "glossolalia" (the unscriptural tongues movement).

When we are established in Christ with a proper doctrinal perspective, we shall fulfill Ephesians 4:14, "That we henceforth be no more children, tossed to and fro, and carried about with every wind of doctrine, by the sleight of men, and cunning craftiness, whereby they lie in wait to deceive."

"Spirit" is *pneuma*. The word as employed here refers to "one in whom a spirit is manifested or embodied, hence one actuated by a spirit, whether divine or demonical."[2]

The apostle Paul sees the source of false doctrine in demons, the energizers of false teachers propagating heresy (1 Tim. 4:1, "devils" should read "demons," from *daimonion*). "Thus these spirits are human beings actuated either by demons or the Holy Spirit. In this case they would be the teachers, pastors and evangelists who circulated around the local churches" (KSW, 159).

The exhortation is that we are to try the spirits to see if they are God-sent. We are to put them to the test. The acid test of Scripture is always, "To the law and to the testimony: if they speak not according to this word, it is because there is no light in them" (Isa. 8:20).

Mealymouthed propagandists of the inclusive ecumenical movement would have us believe that all is well these days and that no one should be labeled "false prophet." They vociferously contend there is no need for doctrinal alarm or excitement. Contrariwise, the Word of God solemnly warns that "many false prophets are gone out into the world." The tense of the verb is perfect, meaning that false prophets "have gone out and they are as a present result in the world of mankind, and they have established themselves amongst the people" (KSW, 160).

> *1 John 4:2, 3.* Hereby know ye the Spirit of God: Every spirit that confesseth that Jesus Christ is come in the flesh is of God:
> And every spirit that confesseth not that Jesus Christ is come in the flesh is not of God: and this is that spirit of antichrist, whereof ye have heard that it should

come; and even now already is it in the world.

The word "confess" is *homologeō*, compounded of *homos*,
"the same," and *legō*, "to speak the same thing as another,"
hence, "to agree with another on some particular thing."
This means that every teacher who is in agreement with the
teaching of the Bible "that Jesus Christ is come in the flesh"
is of God.

A question here is in order.

> What is involved in the statement, "Jesus Christ is
> come in the flesh"? The name "Jesus" is the English
> form of the Greek *Iēsous*, and this is the Greek form of
> the Hebrew name "Jehoshua" which means "Jehovah
> saves." "Christ" is from *christos*, "The Anointed One."
> The words "is come" are in the perfect tense in the
> Greek text. From the foregoing it follows that the state-
> ment speaks of the God of the Old Testament who in
> the Person of His Son became incarnate in human
> flesh without its sin, died on the Cross to satisfy the
> just demands of His law which man broke, and raised
> Himself from the dead in the body in which He died, to
> become the living Saviour of the sinner who places his
> faith in Him in view of what He did for him on
> Calvary's Cross. The person who teaches that, John
> says, is actuated by the Holy Spirit. Likewise, the
> teacher who does not agree to that doctrine is not of
> God. He is actuated by the spirit of Antichrist who
> denies and is against all that the Bible teaches regard-
> ing the person and work of the Lord Jesus. *This is
> modernism* (KSW, 160, 161).

The contextual denial of Christ refers to the Gnostics who
disavowed our Lord's virgin birth. The Gnostics were divid-
ed into two groups:
1. The Docetic Gnostics held that our Lord's human body
was not real, saying that He had only a "phantom body," that
is, a body that only seemed to be real.

2. The Cerinthian Gnostics denied the union of the two na-
tures of our Lord, human and divine, prior to His baptism.
The wicked, twisted-doctrinal offspring of the ancient Gnostics are the present-day modernists and liberals who deny
Christ's virgin birth. All those who deny the virgin birth of
Christ and His sinless deity are classified in Scripture as
deceitful handlers of the Word (2 Cor. 4:2); "false apostles"
and "deceitful workers" (2 Cor. 11:13); tireless seekers of the
plaudits of people (Gal. 1:10); swerving, jangling, fable-
speaking ministers (1 Tim. 1:4, 6); blasphemers (1 Tim. 1:20);
seducers (1 Tim. 4:1); profane, vain babblers (1 Tim. 6:20);
users of unprofitable words (2 Tim. 2:14); "false accusers"
and "despisers of those that are good" (2 Tim. 3:3); men
pleasers (2 Tim. 4:3); lovers of filthy lucre (Titus 1:11). All
such we must know, mark, reject and avoid. Their polluted
doctrine is likened unto death-dealing gangrenous infection
(2 Tim. 2:17). Therefore, we must all the more fervently and
faithfully preach the wholesome words of sound doctrine
(Titus 2:7).

> *1 John 4:4.* Ye are of God, little children, and have over-
> come them: because greater is he that is in you, than
> he that is in the world.

It is an unshakable reality that we now belong to God. We
are His redeemed possession, purchased out of the slave-
market of sin (1 Cor. 6:20; Gal. 3:13; 1 Pet. 1:18-20). We belong
to Him through the unchanging right of redemption. He has
an inheritance in us, described as "the riches of the glory of
his inheritance in the saints" (Eph. 1:18).

Not only are we the "little children" of God by faith in the
finished work of the Lord Jesus upon the cross, but we are
also overcomers of those who hold to false and evil doc-
trines, duped and deceived cohorts of the devil, the archcorrupter of the truth of the gospel.

We do not, of course, overcome in our own strength and
power, but we are overcomers "because greater is he that is

in you, than he that is in the world." May the Lord help us to remember that our strength is in Him (Ps. 27:1; Phil. 4:13). God forbid that we should ever trade His power and strength for human wisdom and understanding. God grant that in these days we may draw by faith upon His power for holy living and victory so that our lives will not be sapped by the devil, who entices us so often with the alluring, golden, glittering things of this world.

> *1 John 4:5.* They are of the world: therefore speak they of the world, and the world heareth them.

This world's system of evil is headed up by Satan, "the prince of the power of the air" (Eph. 2:2). The slimy corruption of this age of evil pervades the whole atmosphere religiously, politically, socially and economically. This age is anti-God, anti-Christ, anti-Bible, anti-prayer and anti-Christian because Satan and his helpers are warring against God. All who are unregenerate are under the dominant sway of this world's malicious prince.

The words, "They are of the world . . . the world heareth them," mean that the unsaved fall easy prey to the false doctrine of the liberals, modernists and cultists who constantly deny the saving efficacy of Christ's atoning blood and substitute a bloodless, hopeless gospel of man's effort. These are frightful times. The hour is late; the need is great. Let us be busy shaking the bushes of our community for people who need to be saved and instructed to attend a sound, Bible-believing gospel church that honors and stands for the whole Word of God. Since this world is heading for inevitable judgment, we need to be busy getting people into the ark of safety according to the terms of the gospel.

> *1 John 4:6.* We are of God: he that knoweth God heareth us; he that is not of God heareth not us. Hereby know we the spirit of truth, and the spirit of error.

What a striking contrast to the world's plight—judgment

apart from the grace of God—are the words, "We are of God." What a wondrous blessing, indeed, that we can know the Lord in redeeming mercy—what condescending love that He knows us! What a glorious spiritual benefit the Lord has lavished profusely upon us, that He has reconciled us to Himself through the miracle of regeneration, making us His people, possession and property.

Those who belong to God know Him. They hear and obey Him. "My sheep hear my voice, and I know them, and they follow me" (John 10:27). Again, "Nevertheless the foundation of God standeth sure, having this seal, The Lord knoweth them that are his. And, Let every one that nameth the name of Christ depart from iniquity" (2 Tim. 2:19). Once more, "The LORD is good, a strong hold in the day of trouble; and he knoweth them that trust in him" (Nahum 1:7).

Spiritual blindness effects deafness to the voice of God, for "he that is not of God heareth not us."

Salvation in the soul brings light and understanding into the heart. God's people are informed people. Correct information is essential to right choice and decision. Wisdom from God through the Word facilitates Scriptural action pleasing to the Lord. It is through the Word that we become grounded in sound doctrine. Since we are of God, we accept the truth and reject error.

CHAPTER XII
THE LOVE OF GOD

We now begin the final division of 1 John, **fellowship with God in love.**

Let us meditate on the fact that the love of God provided the Savior to save us from our sin and that His love in our hearts enables us to love both God and one another (1 John 4:7-21).

> *1 John 4:7.* Beloved, let us love one another: for love is of God; and every one that loveth is born of God, and knoweth God.

"Beloved" refers to Christians, those loved of God, blessed recipients of His redemptive mercy. The Lord lavishes profusely the blessing and glory of His love upon our hearts in unmerited grace. In turn, we are to practice loving fellow believers with this same kind of love—fervently, with pure hearts. In this manner we overtly demonstrate that we have been born of God. To be born of God means that we now have the very life and nature of God (2 Pet. 1:4).

> *1 John 4:8.* He that loveth not knoweth not God; for God is love.

Can we imagine putting an ocean into a teaspoon without it overflowing? Likewise, the love of God in our hearts has an inevitable way of expressing itself in our thoughts, deeds and acts. If one does not give evidence of this love in his life it is a strong indication that he is a total stranger to God's love. Believing in Christ as Savior results in the new birth which in turn results in the Holy Spirit implanting God's love in our hearts (Rom. 5:5). This love must surely come to light.

The words "God is love" mean that God as to His nature is love—God has a loving nature.

> *1 John 4:9.* In this was manifested the love of God toward us, because that God sent his only begotten Son into the world, that we might live through him.

The act of God in sending the Lord Jesus into the world proved His love for us. The Person Who came to Bethlehem to be born of a virgin was God's only begotten Son, the Lord Jesus, "very God of very God," the earthly Son of a divine Father and the heavenly Son of a human mother, preexistent, eternal, holy, righteous, the unspeakable gift of Heaven's fullness to earth's emptiness. What condescending grace when the Sovereign of the skies became the Savior of men. The Lord Jesus came for only one purpose: ". . . to seek and to save that which was lost" (Luke 19:10). He came to deliver from death, to redeem from ruin, to save from sin, to reconcile rebels, to give Heaven's citizenship to aliens of earth.

> *1 John 4:10.* Herein is love, not that we loved God, but that he loved us, and sent his Son to be the propitiation for our sins.

The words "he loved" are in a construction that gives a panoramic view of God's love for the human race. God has always loved sinners. The word "sent" marks the incarnation of our Lord, an historic event. "Propitiation" translates *hilasmos,* which refers to that sacrifice that fully satisfies the demands of the broken law. It was our Lord's death on Calvary's cross. What amazing love our Lord demonstrated for us that we might live through Him. He gave up a throne for a tree, surrendered the wonders of Heaven for the woes of earth, laid aside the crown for the cross, left the palaces of glory for a gory world.

> *1 John 4:11.* Beloved, if God so loved us, we ought also to love one another.

The story of God's wonderful love continues in this verse, in which there are five words that epitomize the story of redemption, "Beloved . . . God so loved us." Those five words are, perhaps, the most important and far-reaching in all the speech of human language. This side of eternity we cannot sound their depth or scale their height or measure their breadth.

> *1 John 4:12.* No man hath seen God at any time. If we love one another, God dwelleth in us, and his love is perfected in us.

The words "No man hath seen God at any time" mean that no one has seen Deity in Its fullest essence. The word "see" is *theaomai*, "to behold, look upon, view attentively, contemplate." God is spirit and, of course, cannot be limited to a man's vision. No one has the mental capacity to behold the fullness of God in His essential nature any more than one could endure the brilliance of the noonday sun from only a few feet away. We should not be discouraged, however, but remember the words of John 1:18, "No man hath seen God at any time; the only begotten Son, which is in the bosom of the Father, he hath declared [revealed] him."

> *1 John 4:13.* Hereby know we that we dwell in him, and he in us, because he hath given us of his Spirit.

Regeneration puts Christ into our hearts; the baptizing work of the Holy Spirit places us in Christ. Being children of God by faith, we live in God and He lives in us. We do not walk the pathway of life alone. The Holy Spirit permanently indwells us, living in our hearts (Rom. 5:5). He is our Helper, Comforter, Teacher and Guide. We shall not fail of our heavenly destiny with the Holy Spirit in us and at our side. He leads us onward and upward to our inheritance in the glory world.

> *1 John 4:14.* And we have seen and do testify that the Father sent the Son to be the Saviour of the world.

Adam, the head of the human race (Rom. 5:12), plunged mankind deep down into the pit of sin and ruin. The wicked, deliberate sin of Adam brought cruel blindness to our eyes and vitiating evil to our hearts, so that the river of rebellion gushed forth its waters of guilt into our souls. In our sin we are said to be aliens, without hope, without Christ and without God in the world (Eph. 2:12). Against this awful background of sin's dark night, the Scriptures declare that Christ came to die for us, to give us life and light, to redeem, to reconcile and to give us sonship in the family of God.

> *1 John 4:15.* Whosoever shall confess that Jesus is the Son of God, God dwelleth in him, and he in God.

The opinions of men will fail. The fading philosophies and whimsical guesses of this world are inadequate. The Scriptures declare with ringing authority that ". . . Jesus is the Son of God." Being the only begotten eternal Son of God, the Lord Jesus is necessarily and exclusively "the way, the truth, and the life" and apart from Him no one can know or go to the Father (John 14:6).

> *1 John 4:16-21.* And we have known and believed the love that God hath to us. God is love; and he that dwelleth in love dwelleth in God, and God in him.
> Herein is our love made perfect, that we may have boldness in the day of judgment: because as he is, so are we in this world.
> There is no fear in love; but perfect love casteth out

fear: because fear hath torment. He that feareth is not made perfect in love.

We love him, because he first loved us.

If a man say, I love God, and hateth his brother, he is a liar: for he that loveth not his brother whom he hath seen, how can he love God whom he hath not seen?

And this commandment have we from him, That he who loveth God love his brother also.

Once we receive the Lord Jesus as Savior, God permanently lives in us and we in Him. What a glorious reality for time and eternity. "And this is life eternal, that they might know thee the only true God, and Jesus Christ, whom thou hast sent" (John 17:3). The powerful love of God in our souls dispels crippling fear, enabling us to love God and the brethren.

The Bible infallibly and trustworthily records the story of God's redemptive mercy. In order that we might have "boldness in the day of judgment," the Lord has abundantly provided for the need of our souls. Our need is threefold. We are:

1. sinners by birth (Rom. 5:12)
2. sinners by practice (Rom. 3:23) and
3. sinners by God's indictment (Rom. 3:19)

God has met our threefold need by providing us with:

1. justification
2. sanctification and
3. glorification

Romans 5:8 summarizes God's love for us, "But God commendeth his love toward us, in that, while we were yet sinners, Christ died for us." Romans 8 is that great chapter of victory that begins with no condemnation and ends with no separation. To be sure, the Lord has done great things for us, heaping upon us the blessings of His salvation.

CHAPTER XIII
MORE THAN CONQUERORS THROUGH CHRIST

1 John 5:1. Whosoever believeth that Jesus is the Christ is born of God: and every one that loveth him that begat loveth him also that is begotten of him.

The greatest experience this side of Glory is to be born of God. "Not by works of righteousness which we have done, but according to his mercy he saved us, by the washing of regeneration, and renewing of the Holy Ghost" (Titus 3:5).

What is involved in believing that Jesus is the Christ? As it relates to our salvation, it means to take ourselves out of our own keeping and to place ourselves in the safe, eternal keeping of the Lord Jesus. As it relates to heresy current in John's day, the teaching refutes the awry doctrine of the Gnostics.

The Cerinthian Gnostics denied the identity of Jesus and the Christ. That is, they denied that the individual whom the Christian Church knew by the name "Jesus" was also the Christ. The word "Christ" is the English spelling of the Greek word *christos* which means "the anointed one." But the predicted Anointed One was to be God-incarnate, virgin-born into the human race. Thus, the incarnation is in view here. But this belief is not a mere intellectual assent to the fact of the incarnation, but a heart acceptance of all that it implied in its purpose, the substitutionary death of the Incarnate

One for sinners, thus making a way of salvation in which God could bestow mercy on the basis of justice satisfied. That person, John says, and he uses the perfect tense here, has been born of God and as a result is a child of God. "Him that begat" is God. "Him that is begotten of Him" is the child of God. . . the person who loves God as his Father also loves God's children because of the fact of the family relationship, that of having a common Father and that of sustaining the relationship, with other believers, that of children in the same family (KSW, 172).

How our souls should be thrilled that our salvation rests not upon empty, powerless creeds but upon the redemptive work of the most wonderful Person in the whole world, our Lord and Savior, Jesus Christ. The poet expressed it:

> I love the Christ of Calvary:
> His life for me He gave.
> He suffered bitter agony
> My sinful soul to save.
>
> Although the sinless Son of God
> He stooped to sin and woe.
> And on the cross He shed His blood
> That washes me white as snow.

1 John 5:2. By this we know that we love the children of God, when we love God, and keep his commandments.

This verse refers back to 1 John 3:14. The words "by this" mean literally "in this." In the very exercise of love toward God, we also have love for the brethren. The love for God and the love for fellow-believers do, in fact, include each other. Each is a test of the other. The word "when" is a key word in the verse. It means more strictly "whenever." It teaches us that our perception of the existence of love to our brethren is developed on every occasion that we exercise love and obedience toward God.

The word "keep" is *tereō,* "to attend to carefully, to take care of, to guard, observe." The word in this connection speaks of a watchful, solicitous guarding and care of God's commandments lest we disobey them, with the thought that we are concerned with His honor and glory and our Christian testimony to the same. It is a jealous safe-keeping of His commandments lest they be violated (KSW, 173).

The words "love" and "keep" are in a construction that speaks of continuous action, emphasizing the truth that constantly obeying and doing the will of God should become a part of our very being.

1 John 5:3. For this is the love of God, that we keep his commandments: and his commandments are not grievous.

Salvation in the heart manifests itself in the life by keeping His commandments. We do not, of course, keep His commandments to be saved but because we are saved.

> I would not work my soul to save
> That work God hath done;
> But I will work like any slave
> For the love of God's dear son.

The words "the love of God" are in a construction that tells us it is "the love for God" in view here. This means that "the saint's love for God is shown by his keeping His commandments. This should be the motivating factor in our keeping God's Word, our love for Him" (KSW, 173). The word for "love" is again *agape,* that divine love produced in the heart of the obedient believer by the Holy Spirit (Rom. 5:5), which love spurs us on to serve the Master with all that we are and all that we have. "Grievous" means "heavy" and denotes that which is "burdensome, severe, stern, violent, cruel, unsparing." Having been set free from the heavy load of sin's guilt, we can render spiritual service to our Lord. "Love for God

makes the keeping of His commandments a delight rather
than a burden" (KSW, 174). Keeping the commandments of
God is keeping and doing His Word. "Love for God lightens
His commandments."[1] Here the words of Matthew 11:29 and
30 come to mind:

> Take my yoke upon you, and learn of me; for I am
> meek and lowly in heart: and ye shall find rest unto
> your souls.
> For my yoke is easy, and my burden is light.

> *1 John 5:4, 5.* For whatsoever is born of God overcom-
> eth the world: and this is the victory that overcometh
> the world, even our faith.
> Who is he that overcometh the world, but he that be-
> lieveth that Jesus is the Son of God?

The reason why God's commandments are not heavy is the
power that comes with the new birth from God. "Whatso-
ever" refers to persons, namely, those persons born of God.
The word "born" speaks of a past completed act of regeneration with the present result that that regenerated individual
has been made a partaker of the divine nature (KSW, 174).
We are now children of God by faith, partakers of the divine
nature (2 Pet. 1:4).

> "Overcometh" is from *nikaō,* "to carry off the victory,
> to come off victorious." The verb implies a battle. Here
> the forces of the world-system of evil, the flesh (totally
> depraved nature), the devil, and the pernicious age-
> system with which the saint is surrounded are all en-
> gaged in a battle against the saint, carrying on an in-
> cessant warfare, the purpose of which is to ruin his
> Christian life and testimony. The verb is in the present
> tense, "is constantly overcoming the world." It is a
> habit of life with the saint to gain victory over the
> world. To go down in defeat is the exception, not the
> rule (KSW, 174).

Yes, to be sure, our victory is in Christ. The word "victory" announces triumph and conquest. "Jesus won the victory over the world (John 16:33) and God in us gives us the victory."[2] Our Lord wrought redemptive victory at the cross and came forth from the sealed sepulchre in resurrection power and glory, defeating Satan, defying death, winning the battle of the ages for man's redemption, causing Satan to suffer stunning shame, declaring with a resounding shout of glory, ". . . All power is given unto me in heaven and in earth" (Matt. 28:18). In Christ alone are we conquering overcomers. The victory over the world, the flesh and the devil is the blessing to all who believe "that Jesus is the Son of God." The shout of victory, "Lord, I believe," from the lips of the healed blind man of John, chapter 9, is also our triumph. All glory belongs to God in the words of the apostle Paul, "But thanks be to God, which giveth us the victory through our Lord Jesus Christ" (1 Cor. 15:57). The world must always smell the dust of defeat, but the child of God may know victory now and forever.

> *1 John 5:6-8.* This is he that came by water and blood, even Jesus Christ; not by water only, but by water and blood. And it is the Spirit that beareth witness, because the Spirit is truth.
> For there are three that bear record in heaven, the Father, the Word, and the Holy Ghost: and these three are one.
> And there are three that bear witness in earth, the spirit, and the water, and the blood: and these three agree in one.

The fundamental concept of the doctrine of salvation is that it is entirely of God, from A to Z. God the Father planned our salvation; God the Son purchased it upon the cross in accordance with the Father's plan; God the Holy Spirit perfects it in our soul as we believe the gospel. The members of the Godhead work together for man's salvation. All things proceed from the Father, through the Son, in the power of the Holy Spirit.

The word "came" in 1 John 5:6 refers to a definite fact in history, namely, the first advent of the Son of God, in which He embraced human nature without its sin through the Virgin Birth. "His coming to make an atonement for sin was accompanied by and made effective through water and blood" (KSW, 175).

> *Water* refers to Christ's baptism at the beginning of His Messianic work, through which He declared His purpose to fulfill all righteousness (Matt. 3:15). *Blood* refers to His bloody death upon the Cross for the sin of the world.[3]
>
> These two incidents in the Incarnation are singled out because at the baptism Jesus was formally set apart to His Messianic work by the coming of the Holy Spirit upon Him and by the Father's audible witness, and because at the cross His work reached its culmination. ("It is finished," Jesus said.)[4]

In verse 8 the same three witnesses of verses 6 and 7 are repeated with the Spirit mentioned first. The words "these three agree in one" mean "the three are for the one thing," "to bring us to faith in Jesus as the Incarnate Son of God, the very purpose for which John wrote his Gospel (20:31)."[5]

CHAPTER XIV
BLESSED ASSURANCE FOREVER

The blessed assurance of our salvation rests surely and solidly upon the infallible Word of God (1 John 5:9-13).

> *1 John 5:9.* If we receive the witness of men, the witness of God is greater: for this is the witness of God which he hath testified of his Son.

The words "if we receive" are in the condition of being assumed as true, better rendered "since we receive." "John's thought is as follows: Since we are in the habit of receiving the testimony of men, the testimony of God is greater and therefore should be received" (KSW, 177). The testimony of God concerns His Son Whom He has given. The word of man in newspapers, radio and legal documents is received without question. In view of the fact that we do believe man's word, can we afford not to believe God?

> We receive the testimony from our fellowman. But God's testimony is greater than man's testimony. God testifies of the fact that He has borne testimony concerning His Son, and since He is the One who has borne this testimony, not man, that testimony should be received. The verb is in the perfect tense, speaking of a past act of bearing testimony with the result that the testimony is on record at the present time (KSW, 177).

1 John 5:10. He that believeth on the Son of God hath the witness in himself: he that believeth not God hath made him a liar; because he believeth not the record that God gave of his Son.

The word "believeth" is *pisteuō*, "to trust in, to adhere to, to rely upon, to place confidence in." The word refers to a strong and welcome conviction or belief that Jesus is the Christ, through Whom we obtain eternal salvation. To believe on the Son of God is to place trust and confidence in the Lord Jesus, to commit one's soul to Him, to have faith in His wonderful power to save the soul. Faith in Christ as Savior opens up the door of salvation, plunges the believer into the cleansing river of grace, opens up the throne room of God's mercy. The words "hath the witness in himself" mean that:

> ... The one who believes on the Son of God has the testimony in him to the effect that he thus believes. Paul in Romans 8:16 tells us that the Holy Spirit bears testimony in connection with our human spirit. . .energized by the Holy Spirit, gives us the consciousness that we as believers are children of God. The Holy Spirit testifies to us that that same thing is true (KSW, 177, 178).

The one who does not believe God, or the infallible record God has given of His Son, makes God a liar. It is a solemn course of evil action not to believe God. Failure to believe God robs the soul of the best gift God has for man, namely, salvation.

1 John 5:11. And this is the record, that God hath given to us eternal life, and this life is in his Son.

The reliable Word of the Lord is that we have eternal life in the Lord Jesus. "And this is life eternal, that they might know thee the only true God, and Jesus Christ, whom thou hast sent" (John 17:3). The words "in Christ" throughout the New Testament speak of our position in grace. Only "in

Christ" are we rightly related to God so as to receive salvation in all its ineffable glory and fullness. Our Lord said, ". . . I am come that they might have life, and that they might have it more abundantly" (John 10:10). Every fundamental believer knows that the Bible emphatically teaches that salvation is in Christ alone, in Whom we are blessed with all spiritual blessings (Eph. 1:3). "Neither is there salvation in any other: for there is none other name under heaven given among men, whereby we must be saved" (Acts 4:12). Eternal life! What a glorious reality—the present possession of every true believer! Mortal tongue cannot describe it anymore than deaf ears can catch the sweet song of a bird. The human mind cannot fully comprehend its ocean-like depth and fullness anymore than clumsy hands can paint a breathtaking sunset. Eternal life is God's life, enduring and unceasing, ever new, ever wonderful and ever satisfying. The greatest gift that God can bestow upon us is making us His children, heirs of God and joint-heirs with Christ, not for a day, month or year but for eternity! Little wonder the poet shouts, "Hallelujah, what a Savior!"

> *1 John 5:12.* He that hath the Son hath life; and he that hath not the Son of God hath not life.

This verse shows unmistakably that one cannot be neutral: he is either in Christ or not in Christ, either for the Lord or against Him.

> He that believeth on him is not condemned: but he that believeth not is condemned already, because he hath not believed in the name of the only begotten Son of God (John 3:18).
> He that believeth on the Son hath everlasting life: and he that believeth not the Son shall not see life; but the wrath of God abideth on him (John 3:36).

The sin question was settled at Calvary nearly two thousand years ago. The issue now is the Son question, "What

will you do with Jesus who is called the Christ?" There are
two ways set before us, the way of death and the way of life.
To receive Christ is to live; to reject Him is to die. "For the
wages of sin is death; but the gift of God is eternal life
through Jesus Christ our Lord" (Rom. 6:23). "And lo a voice
from heaven, saying, This is my beloved Son, in whom I am
well pleased" (Matt. 3:17). What a wonderful privilege God
affords us that we can know His Son and thus have life, so
we can walk the pathway of redemptive mercy to Heaven.
The purpose of John's Gospel is given in these words:

> But these are written, that ye might believe that Jesus
> is the Christ, the Son of God; and that believing ye
> might have life through his name (John 20:31).

> *1 John 5:13.* These things have I written unto you that
> believe on the name of the Son of God; that ye may
> know that ye have eternal life, and that ye may believe
> on the name of the Son of God.

Quite often the question comes, "Can a person really know
for sure that he is saved?" The Bible has the answer. Yes, we
can know for sure *now* that we are saved *forever.* Our hope
in Christ is an unquestionable certainty, a glorious reality
beyond the reach of failure. "Which hope we have as an an-
chor of the soul, both sure and stedfast . . ." (Heb. 6:19). The
word "know" speaks of absolute, beyond-the-peradventure-
of-a-doubt knowledge, a positive knowledge. The Lord wants
us to know that we have an anchored hope in Christ, that we
are saved forever, that the blessed assurance of our salvation
is now a present possession, not a future dim uncertainty. All
of this is expressed in the words, "that ye may know that ye
have eternal life." Believing in the security of the believer
brings spiritual joy and triumph to our hearts. Fear cripples
and hinders our spiritual progress. Yes, in Christ we have a
perfect—that is, a completed, finished—salvation. The Word
of God is infallible, forever settled in Heaven (Ps. 119:89). The
nature of God is unchangeable (Mal. 3:6). The counsel of God

is immutable (Heb. 6:17). Therefore, the salvation of God is perfect, because the Lord Jesus Himself is the Author and Finisher of our faith (Heb. 12:2). Think of it! For now and forever we can simply and fully rely upon Jesus, Who has purchased an everlasting salvation by the shedding of His own precious blood (1 Pet. 1:18, 19). Therefore, the abiding safety of the believer's soul is certain, resting with an omnipotent God who will see to its fulfillment and our safe arrival in Glory.

CHAPTER XV
CONFIDENCE IN PRAYER

Prayer is the ordained means of God by which He supplies the needs of His people (1 John 5:14-21).

> *1 John 5:14, 15.* And this is the confidence that we have in him, that, if we ask any thing according to his will, he heareth us:
> And if we know that he hear us, whatsoever we ask, we know that we have the petitions that we desired of him.

A reputable Bible scholar has listed Numbers 7:89 as an excellent verse on the definition of prayer:

> And when Moses was gone into the tabernacle of the congregation to speak with him, then he heard the voice of one speaking unto him from off the mercy seat that was upon the ark of testimony, from between the two cherubims: and he spake unto him.

Prayer is a holy privilege by means of which we talk with God and He speaks to us. Prayer is a spiritual exercise profitable to the soul, uplifting to the spirit and joyful to the heart. One of the names of God is "O thou that hearest prayer" (Ps. 65:2). Prayer ought to become a part of us. The place of prayer is the place of power. Prayerlessness means powerlessness. If we would have power with men, we must have power with God in prayer. Most of our failures, heartaches and griefs are attributable to prayerlessness. How foolish to neglect prayer when the Word teaches us that "The eyes of the LORD are upon the righteous, and his ears are open unto their cry" (Ps. 34:15). A praying church is a going, growing, glowing church. Revivals are not worked up but prayed down.

The word "confidence" in 1 John 5:14 is *parresia*, "free and fearless confidence, cheerful courage, boldness, assurance." The phrase "in him" means literally "toward him," speaking of the saint's attitude toward a prayer-hearing and a prayer-answering God. "Ask" is *aiteō*, "to ask for something to be given." The thought here is "to keep on asking for something for ourselves" (KSW, 179). The first fundamental considera-tion in praying is that we must pray according to the will of God, expressed in the words that the Lord hears us when we ask "according to his will." As we pray and trust God we learn how to pray in the school of prayer. " 'We have our re-quests' not always as we pray but as we would pray were we wiser. God gives us not what we ask but what we really need" (KSW, 179). Often the following words are a real com-fort to our hearts in the matter of prayer: "Likewise the Spir-it also helpeth our infirmities: for we know not what we should pray for as we ought: but the Spirit itself maketh in-tercession for us with groanings which cannot be uttered" (Rom. 8:26).

> *1 John 5:16, 17.* If any man see his brother sin a sin which is not unto death, he shall ask, and he shall give him life for them that sin not unto death. There is a sin unto death: I do not say that he shall pray for it.
> All unrighteousness is sin: and there is a sin not unto death.

The Bible commands us to pray for one another. Interces-sory praying is a spiritual exercise of tremendous value to our hearts and lives. However, we are told not to pray for those who have committed "the sin unto death." What is "the sin unto death"? There are differences of opinion on this difficult verse. The Bible-taught student is well aware that the final court of appeals for determining the meaning of Scripture is the context. A conclusion contrary to the context will result in confusion and frustration. The solemn warning is to believers who might commit "a sin unto death" and thus expose themselves to the judgment of God.

Living in persistent disobedience and stubbornly refusing to confess and forsake known sins that dishonor Christ and weaken the church's testimony puts the believer in the place where God will deal with him. The believer must practice keeping short accounts with God, confessing and forsaking his sins on a regular basis. He must be sure he is walking in daily fellowship with the Lord, delighting in the full blessing of God. Our goal should always be to walk in the pathway of holiness, honoring the Lord in thought, word and deed.

The Word of God warns the child of God about the terrible consequences of unconfessed sins. Psalm 66:18 states, "If I regard iniquity in my heart, the Lord will not hear me." The term "regard" means "to look at with favor." Wise is the believer who will turn from his sin instead of taking pleasure in it.

In Proverbs 28:13 we read about the wickedness of covering up sin, "He that covereth his sins shall not prosper: but whoso confesseth and forsaketh them shall have mercy." The true confession of one's sins brings the cleansing and forgiving work of God into our lives. Commenting on the words, "a sin unto death," in 1 John 5:16, Dr. Charles Ryrie says, "Believers can sin to the point where physical death results as the judgment of God (cf. 1 Cor. 11:30). The Greek reads *sin*, not *a sin*, (italics his) in vv. 16 and 17."[1] The word for "death" is *thanatos* and denotes physical death; namely, that separation of the soul and spirit from the body by which the life on earth ends. Regarding "sin unto death" Merrill Unger says, "Both Saul and Samson are types of this very severe chastening in the Old Testament. This sin is *not to be prayed for* (italics his) because it involves the execution of an immutable law of God unaltered by prayer, 16c. Sin has different degrees of seriousness, 17."[2]

Many years ago, a young man by the name of Vince Foster suddenly catapulted to boxing fame by winning a number of welter-weight fights. A friend witnessed to him and led him to faith in Christ. Afterwards, at the beginning of each boxing match, Foster would give his testimony of faith in Christ as Savior and Lord. However, he soon backslid and lost his testimony and became careless about living for the Lord. On his way home from Chicago to Omaha one night, driving intoxicated, he ran his auto under the back of a large truck and was killed instantly. Vince Foster had evidently committed "sin unto death."

> *1 John 5:18.* We know that whosoever is born of God sinneth not; but he that is begotten of God keepeth himself, and that wicked one toucheth him not.

> "We know" is *oida*, "to have positive, absolute knowledge." "Is born" is in the perfect tense, and speaks of a past complete act of regeneration with the present result that the believing sinner is a born-one of God. "Sinneth" is present tense, continuous action. The one born of God does not keep on habitually sinning. The believer does not practice sin. "Is begotten" is aorist tense and speaks of the Son of God, Son of God by eternal generation from God the Father in a birth that never took place because it always was. "Keepeth" is *tereō*, "to take care of, to guard." The word expresses "watchful care" (KSW, 182).

The Lord Jesus keeps us day by day by His infinite power on our way to the City of God.

> "Wicked one" is *poneros*, "evil in active opposition to the good, pernicious." The word refers to Satan who is not content to perish in his own corruption, but seeks

to drag everyone else down with himself to his final doom. "Toucheth" is *haptō*, ... "to grasp, to lay hold of." The meaning of the word here is that the Lord holds on to us. "Himself" is *autos*, ... should be rendered "him."

As Smith says, "There is no comfort in the thought that we are in our own keeping; our security is not in our grip on Christ but His grip on us." [Here is a translation of 1 John 5:18:]

We know absolutely that everyone who has been born out of God and as a result is a regenerated individual, does not keep on habitually sinning. But He who was born out of God maintains a watchful guardianship over him, and the Pernicious One does not lay hold of him (KSW, 183).

1 John 5:19. And we know that we are of God, and the whole world lieth in wickedness.

The words "we know that we are of God" speak of the truth that we have a certain absolute knowledge that we belong to God. We are His possession. Children of God by faith, we have eternal life in God's Son (1 John 5:12). God also has an inheritance in us (Eph. 1:18). "Lieth" indicates the passive, unprogressive state of the unsaved in the sphere of Satan's influence. "World" is *kosmos*, the world-system of evil in active opposition to God, headed up by the devil, the prince of the power of the air (Eph. 2:2), of which the unsaved are a part. "Wickedness" is again *poneros*, same word translated "wicked one" in verse 19, and refers to Satan. Dr. R. A. Torrey once said, "The whole world lies in the lap of the devil."

1 John 5:20. And we know that the Son of God is come, and hath given us an understanding, that we may know him that is true, and we are in him that is true, even in his Son Jesus Christ. This is the true God, and eternal life.

This verse reminds us at once of John 17:3, "And this is life eternal, that they might know thee the only true God, and Jesus Christ, whom thou hast sent."

> This verse is the assurance and guarantee of it all—the incarnation, an overwhelming demonstration of God's interest in us and His concern for our highest good. "Our faith is not a matter of intellectual theory but of personal and growing acquaintance with God through the enlightenment of Christ's Spirit."
> "Is come" is *hekō*, "to have come, have arrived, be present." John does not use *erchomai* here, a verb which speaks only of the act of coming, but *hekō*, which includes in the idea of coming, sense of personal presence, the fact of arrival and personal presence. It is, "the Son of God has come (in incarnation), has arrived and is here." "While He departed in His glorified body to Heaven, yet He is here in His Presence in the Church. His coming was not like that of a meteor, flashing across the sky and then gone. He remains in His followers on earth." "Hath given" is perfect in tense, "has given with the result that the gift is in the permanent possession of the recipient." "True" is not *alethes*, "true," that is, veracious, but *alēthinos*, "genuine" as opposed to the false and counterfeit, here, the genuine God as opposed to the false God of the heretics (KSW, 183, 184).

1 John 5:21. Little children, keep yourselves from idols.

"Little children" is *teknia*, a tender term of endearment, often used in the epistle. It means "little born-ones." "Keep" is *phulassō*, "to guard, to watch, to keep watch." The world is watching us constantly. We must ever keep watch over what we say and do. The word was used of the garrison of a city guarding it against attack from the enemy. "The heart is a citadel, and it must be guarded against insidious assailants from without, for out of the heart are the issues of life"

(KSW, 184). "Idols" is *eidōlōn,* "an image, likeness, idol." The Apostle John is thinking, not of the heathen worship of Ephesus—Artemis and her Temple, but of the heretical substitutes for the Christian conception of God. He had just written concerning the genuine God of the Bible. Now he warns against the false, counterfeit gods of paganism" (KSW, 184). We must ever guard against anything that occupies the place of God and that hinders spiritual progress.

NOTES

Chapter I

1. James M. Gray, *Synthetic Bible Study* (New York: Fleming H. Revell, 1906), 318.

Chapter II

1. Henry Alford, *Alford's Greek New Testament,* vol. 4 (Cambridge, MA: Deighton, Bell and Company, 1871), 426.
2. Unless otherwise noted, all quotes from Kenneth S. Wuest are from his book *In These Last Days* (Grand Rapids: Wm. B. Eerdmans Publishing Company, 1954) and will be indicated by the author's initials (KSW) and the page numbers. Used with permission.
3. Alford, 426.

Chapter IV

1. A. T. Robertson, *Word Pictures in the New Testament,* vol. 6 (Nashville: Broadman Press, 1931), 209.
2. W. Robertson Nichol, *The Expositor's Greek New Testament,* vol. 5 (Grand Rapids: Wm. B. Eerdmans Publishing Company, 1956), 173.
3. Robertson, 209.

Chapter V

1. Robertson, 210.

2. Ibid.
3. Ibid., 212.

Chapter VI

1. Joseph Thayer, *A Greek-English Lexicon of the New Testament* (Chicago: American Book Company, 1889), 25.
2. Nichol, 178.

Chapter VII

1. Marvin Vincent, *Word Studies in the New Testament*, vol. 2 (Grand Rapids: Wm. B. Eerdmans Publishing Company, 1957), 339.
2. John Lineberry, *Salvation Is of the Lord* (Grand Rapids: Zondervan Publishing Company, 1959), 92, 93.

Chapter VIII

1. Vincent, 344.
2. Ibid., 346.
3. John Lineberry, "The Sinless Savior," *Baptist Bulletin* (October 1963), 8.
4. Robertson, 222.

Chapter IX

1. Kenneth S. Wuest, *Philippians through Revelation: An Expanded Translation* (Grand Rapids: Wm. B. Eerdmans Publishing Company, 1959), n.p.

Chapter XI

1. Robertson, 229.
2. Thayer, 522.

Chapter XIII

1. Robertson, 239.
2. Ibid., 238.
3. Vincent, 365.

4. Robertson, 239.
5. Ibid., 241.

Chapter XV

1. Charles C. Ryrie, *The Ryrie Study Bible* (Chicago: Moody Press, 1976), notes on 1 John 5:16.
2. Merrill F. Unger, *Unger's Bible Handbook* (Chicago: Moody Press, 1966), 829.

BIBLIOGRAPHY

Alford, Henry. *Alford's Greek New Testament.* 4 vols. Cambridge, MA: Deighton, Bell and Company, 1871.

Gray, James M. *Synthetic Bible Study.* New York: Fleming H. Revell, 1906.

Lineberry, John. *Salvation Is of the Lord,* Grand Rapids: Zondervan Publishing Company, 1959.

Nichol. W. Robertson. *The Expositor's Greek New Testament.* 5 vols. Grand Rapids; Wm. B. Eerdmans Publishing Company, 1956.

Robertson, A. T. *Word Pictures in the New Testament.* 6 vols. Nashville: Broadman Press, 1931.

Ryrie, Charles C. *The Ryrie Study Bible.* Chicago: Moody Press, 1976.

Thayer, Joseph. *A Greek-English Lexicon of the New Testament,* Chicago: American Book Company, 1889.

Unger, Merrill F. *Unger's Bible Handbook.* Chicago: Moody Press, 1966.

Vincent, Marvin. *Word Studies in the New Testament.* 4 vols. Grand Rapids: Wm. B. Eerdmans Publishing Company, 1957.

Wuest, Kenneth S. *In These Last Days, II Peter, I, II, III, John, and Jude in The Greek New Testament.* Grand Rapids: Wm. B. Eerdmans Publishing Company, 1954.

_____. *Philippians through Revelation, an Expanded Translation.* Grand Rapids: Wm. B. Eerdmans Publishing Company, 1959.